AUSTRALIA IN STYLE

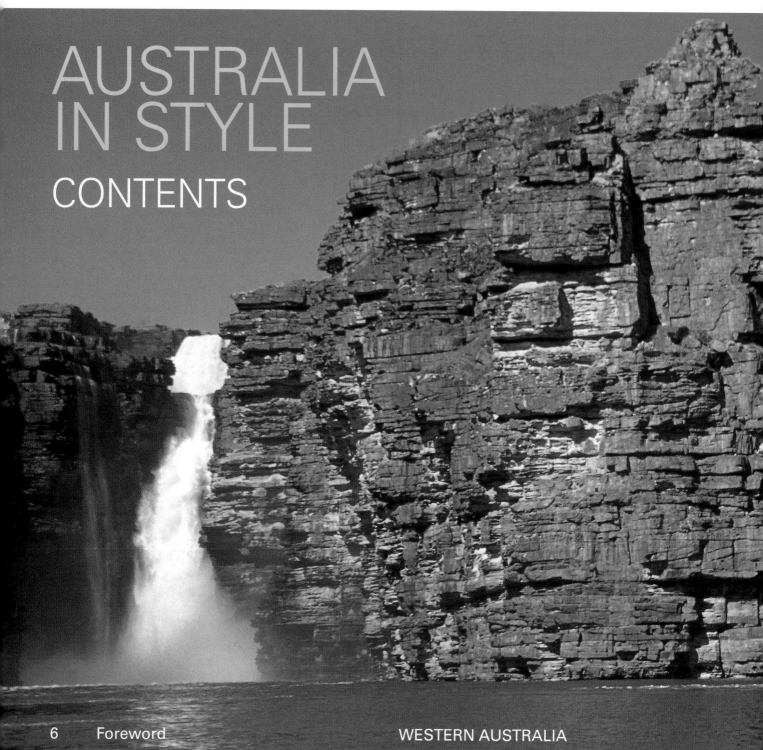

AUSTRALIA IN STYLE
CONTENTS

AUSTRALIA IN STYLE

TEXT AND PHOTOGRAPHY
Michael Gebicki
with additional material from Tim Dub

GRAPHIC DESIGN
Shannon O'Neill
Robert Boesch

PRODUCTION
Mathew Peden

R.M. WILLIAMS PUBLISHING TEAM
Tanya Buchanan
Therese Hall
Sophie Herron
Mark Muller
Paul Myers
Maxine Romilly
Janine Wassens

SCANNING AND PROOFING
Ultra Colour

PRINTING
SNP Security Printing

DISTRIBUTION
Gordon & Gotch

PUBLISHED BY
Outback Publishing Company
ABN 92 113 405 157
A partnership between
R.M. Williams Publishing Pty Ltd
ACN 068 461 263
and Project Publishers Pty Ltd
ACN 082 813 287
In association with Outback Encounter

Level 11, 52 Alfred Street
Milsons Point, NSW, 2061 Australia

Telephone +61 2 9028 5400
Facsimile +61 2 9028 5431

Email subscribe@rmwilliams.com.au

Website www.outbackmag.com.au

ISBN 0-9579709-6-X

RRP $24.95

FOREWORD

AUSTRALIA, OR AS some would say, *Terra Australis*, is unique in many ways, above all else in its combination of modernity and style with light and space. It is unlike any other as the only continent in the world occupied by one nation-state, but also because statistically it does have more light and space than any other continent or country.

With so much to offer, over the decades a number of representations have emerged, giving a certain typecasting to parts of Australia, but now is the time to add to existing imagery, now is the time to challenge the romantic, rustic notions of outback Australia, and indeed parts of coastal Australia.

In a truly excellent way *Australia in Style* examines a wide range of what this great country has to offer at the start of the 21st century, recognising many of the extra components now available, often where you least expect them.

Enter from stage right the architects, engineers and entrepreneurs of the 21st century creating a whole new level of comfort and serenity and serendipity. Enter from stage left the better of the town planners, bureaucrats and local, state and federal governmental leaders who are beavering away at getting the template right, in particular the infrastructure right.

On stage centre, if you like, are our two greatest assets, our natural or physical attributes and our dynamic people. Bringing all of this together, you have the outstanding results displayed in this publication in many beautiful ways. For all that the romantic and rustic have a role to play, this image must be balanced by the modernity and diversity and style available across the continent.

Take for example the magnificence of a steam locomotive in South Australia hauling the *Afghan Express* from Port Augusta to Quorn to Pichi Richi Pass, paralleling on part of the journey the east-west and north-south mainline where the internationally

renowned long-distance trains, the *Indian Pacific* and *The Ghan*, convey passengers on transcontinental journeys.

Just when you thought you were into cappuccino and latte withdrawal-symptom panic, halfway between Port Augusta and Quorn the *Afghan Express* pauses, you alight and enter The Willows restaurant, to behold steam arising from the coffee machine producing plenty of cappuccinos et al.

In the middle of Carnarvon Gorge in central Queensland you will suddenly come across five-star safari tents, equally in coastal hamlet after coastal hamlet right around the mainland and Tasmania, again when you least expect it, lo and behold sensationally designed bed and breakfast accommodation awaits.

Australia in Style is all about the mixture that constitutes Australia in the opening years of the 21st century, effecting great progress, but also increasing harmony with the environment and climatic factors. Current political debates and economic reporting often paint outback Australia and country Australia especially as somewhat negative areas lacking in profitable enterprises and dominated by the falling-down farm sheds, the rusty machinery, the empty houses and derelict railway stations.

The truth of the matter is that there are many dynamic profit centres buried away in country towns large and small, from Victoria's Beechworth Bakery to the Nundle woollen mills in New South Wales, and of course on just about every well-managed farm and grazing property, despite what the whinging elements might say. Equally, there are many dynamic people to be met downtown in our capital cities, but just as many in the back of beyond. The entrepreneurs who developed many of the attractions presented in this book reflect this.

All in all, enjoy the publication forthwith, but then go out and enjoy what tickles your fancy from the magnificent presentations that follow.

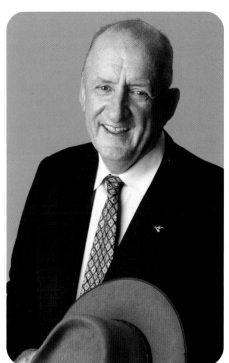

TIM FISCHER
CHAIR, TOURISM AUSTRALIA,
FORMER DEPUTY PRIME MINISTER

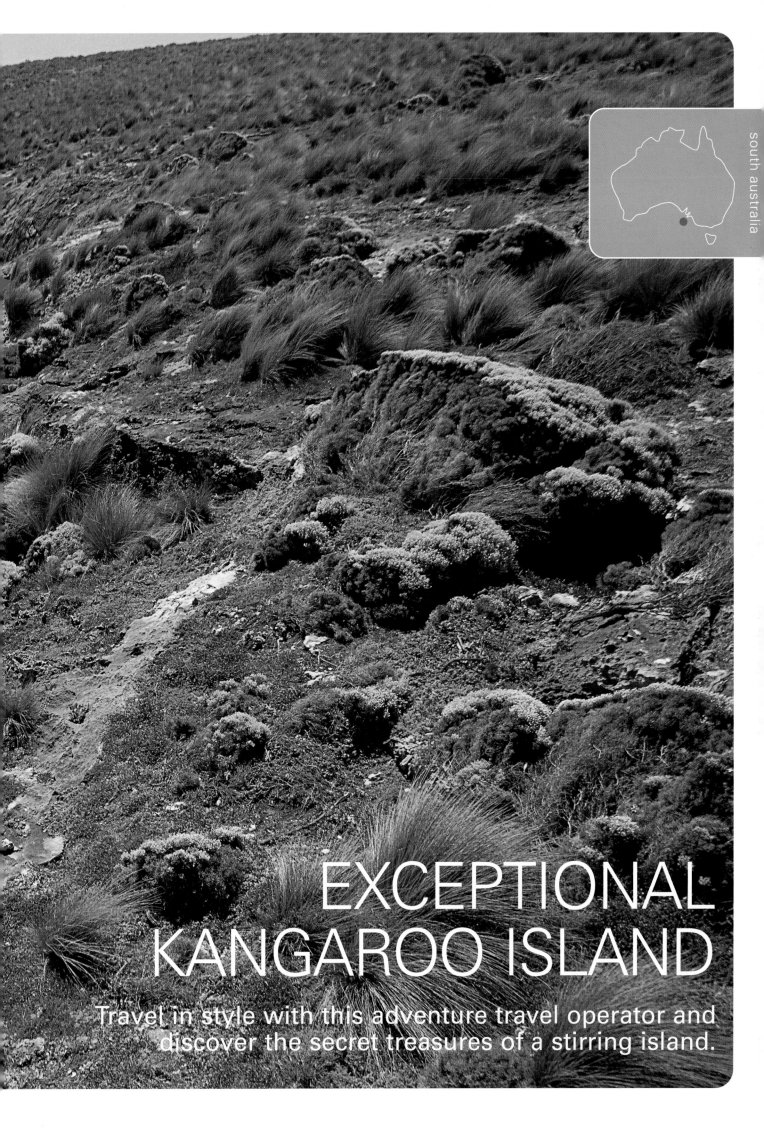

EXCEPTIONAL KANGAROO ISLAND

Travel in style with this adventure travel operator and discover the secret treasures of a stirring island.

Kangaroo Island – teeming with wildlife wonders. Expert guides who know where to find the island's wonders also know how to rustle up a super barbeque lunch when the heat is on.

Even for most Australians, seeing wildlife in the wild is a rare experience – which is what makes Kangaroo Island so special.

AUSTRALIA'S NATIVE PLANTS and animals are among nature's strangest creations. So otherworldly are the life forms that hop, crawl and slither across Australia's surface that for many years scientists thought that they had a completely different evolutionary origin from the rest of the planet's species – a separate creation. But as remarkable as they are, many Australian animals are also elusive.

Just 16 kilometres off South Australia's southern coast and a 30-minute flight from Adelaide, Kangaroo Island – KI to the locals – is a repository of Australian wildlife. Its very separateness has insulated it against rabbits, foxes and feral cats, and as a result the whole island resonates with the sights and sounds of wild Australia. If you want to see koalas, kangaroos, echidnas, platypus and sea lions in their native habitat, there is nowhere else that comes close to Kangaroo Island.

While Kangaroo Island has everything you need for the do-it-yourself explorer – including a good network of roads and well-signposted attractions – there are several reasons why you need to take a guided tour, and the best is insider knowledge. Kangaroo Island does not give up its secret treasures to just anyone. Just a two-minute drive from the airport, for example, is a colony of koalas that lives in the manna gums. At the wheel of your hire car, it's easy to whiz through without seeing anything more than a shady grove of towering trees – yet it would be a shame to miss the koalas. Even among Australians, there are not many who will ever see a koala in the wild. It takes an expert guide to point out the bundle of sticks high on a cliff that marks a sea eagle's

nest, locate the V-shaped furrow on the water that identifies a swimming platypus, introduce you to the wallabies and kangaroos of the Lathami Conservation Park – or conjure up wild koalas on cue. And if you want to experience the island's best, no other tour operator does it quite like Exceptional Kangaroo Island.

Originally established in 1986 as a diving and fishing charter operator, and trading as Adventure Charters of Kangaroo Island, Exceptional Kangaroo Island is firmly established as one of Australia's premier wildlife tour operators.

From the beginning, the company's founder, Craig Wickham, has been crafting a very special experience for small numbers of visitors to the island. He has assembled a small team of dedicated, sharp-eyed, outdoor enthusiasts who combine the roles of naturalists, historians, drivers, guides and storytellers, each with an expert's knowledge of the island's plants, animals and people, plus a rich fund of stories of island life.

Come lunchtime and those same guides become expert chefs, with the ability to concoct a delicious fish barbeque, while guests enjoy a well-chilled bottle of South Australian wine in one of the secret places reserved exclusively for guests of Exceptional Kangaroo Island.

A deluxe four-wheel-drive experience that slays the tyranny of distance.

IF YOU WANT to make the most of your time on the island. Exceptional has a choice of off-the-shelf tours, which can be anything from the one-day Overnight Adventure to the Kangaroo Island Wanderer – a three-day package with plenty of time to hike, explore a little more intensively on your own or spend a day out fishing. All of these tours and activities can be provided as a shared group experience or a private tour, which gives you the freedom to determine the itinerary, and to spend as long as you like admiring the sea lions, or waiting for the perfect light on the Remarkable Rocks.

The company can also tailor special-interest experiences to suit individual requirements. Just some of the possible themes include bird-watching, mammal excursions, photographic safaris, historic sites, nocturnal wildlife-watching, wildflower tours and geological expeditions. Previous clients for such tours have included The American Museum of Natural History, the National Audubon Society and San Diego Zoo.

Exceptional uses a fleet of four-wheel-drive vehicles for its tours, based on the Toyota chassis, some with specially modified bodies that provide extra spacious seating. Whichever vehicle you're aboard, you'll get rugged, dependable transport with the ability to take you to any road on the island in style and comfort, with easy access and a big window with a box-seat view.

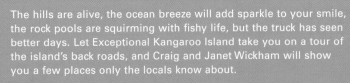

The hills are alive, the ocean breeze will add sparkle to your smile, the rock pools are squirming with fishy life, but the truck has seen better days. Let Exceptional Kangaroo Island take you on a tour of the island's back roads, and Craig and Janet Wickham will show you a few places only the locals know about.

KI's coastline is a mixture of reefs and beaches. The Remarkable Rocks live up to their name, but a sea pool is all the fascination a child needs.

Allow several days to properly explore Kangaroo Island's many natural attractions.

OUTBACK ENCOUNTER PORTFOLIO MEMBER

KANGAROO ISLAND IS big. Sprawling 145 kilometres from east to west and about 60km from top to bottom, it demands time. A single day is barely enough to take in the highlights, but this is an experience to savour, and the slower you go, the more you'll discover. Two days is a sensible minimum.

While the headline attractions are glaringly obvious, there is a substrata of simple pleasures that demand time, such as poking about in rock pools, or watching an osprey soaring along the cliffs at D'Estrees Bay.

High among the island's stellar attractions is Seal Bay, where guided groups of visitors stroll along the beach just a few metres from the sea lions as they rest, cavort, bellow and occasionally,

fight. Another highlight is the Remarkable Rocks, where the elements have carved granite rocks into fantastic shapes, like the vertebrae of some prehistoric giant. Even KI's vegetation is different. One of the distinctive features of its landscape is its grass trees, black stumps which sprout a clump of long, flexible green filaments.

Something else that sets KI apart is the people who live there. The island attracts some truly amazing talents, and its permanent population of around 4000 includes a substantial colony of writers and artists – as well as sheep farmers, fishermen, cheesemakers and beekeepers. A supremely relaxed crew who firmly believe that they live in paradise – and after a few days, you'll probably agree.

EXCEPTIONAL KANGAROO ISLAND

LOCATION: Kangaroo Island is 120 kilometres south-west of Adelaide.

GETTING THERE: Emu Airways operates several flights daily between Adelaide and Kingscote, the main town on Kangaroo Island. Flight time is about 30 minutes. Sealink ferries make up to 12, 45-minute crossings between Cape Jervis and Penneshaw each day.

WHAT'S INCLUDED: Pickup from accommodation or airport, all admission fees, lunch and snacks.

MAKING THE MOST OF IT: Take sturdy footwear and a warm, waterproof jacket.

CONTACT: Outback Encounter
33 Queen Street, Thebarton
South Australia, 5031, Australia
Telephone + 61 8 **8354 4405**
Facsimile + 61 8 **8354 4406**
Email info@outbackencounter.com
Website www.outbackencounter.com

ANGORICHINA STATION

Sample the daily working lives of a
remarkable Flinders Ranges pastoral family.

Di and Ian Fargher's home is an oasis of beauty and calm among the wild majesty of the Flinders, an area in which Ian's family has run pastoral operations for four generations.

Cradled by rough, rocky hills this 650 square-kilometre sheep station is the perfect place to sample life on a working outback property.

IF YOU WANT to experience outback Australia in all its rugged glory, there are few places that compare with the Central Flinders Ranges of South Australia. Stretching north from the armpit of the Spencer Gulf, this chain of desert mountains has a stark, surreal beauty all its own. The pine trees that die and shed their limbs in a histrionic parody of grief, the rocky hills that glow like hot coals in the late afternoon, the wildflowers that appear as if by magic after rain – the Central Flinders has a biblical quality that has made it a favourite with filmmakers, painters and photographers.

Angorichina Station brings something extra special to the equation. Cradled by rough, rocky hills near the village of Blinman, this 650 square-kilometre sheep station is the perfect place to sample life on a working outback property, and to share in the lives of the remarkable people who call it home.

Ian Fargher, who owns Angorichina with his wife, Di, is the fourth generation of his family to run sheep on this station. This is severe country, a wild, barren, semi-desert where each sheep requires 15 acres to survive, although in times of drought that ratio can triple. For guests, one of the real pleasures of staying at Angorichina is the chance to become absorbed into the life of a working outback sheep station. There are horses to be fed, machinery to be maintained and always a to-do list that fills every daylight hour. Operating the station and managing the sheep that roam across its vast open spaces calls for a level of independence that is beyond the wildest dreams

of most urbanites. From generating their own power to pumping water to carving out roads, flying an aircraft and maintaining their equipment, this is a lesson in rugged self-sufficiency, involving qualities of ingenuity, perseverance and – when all else fails – brute strength. Yet Di and Ian also maintain a level of sophistication and a taste for the finer things in life that seem almost unbelievable in these harsh surroundings.

Angorichina also has a proud history. Set apart from the homestead, the shearing shed and its outbuildings – shearers' quarters, the former manager's residence, bridle room, windmills and the numberless small sheds that a working station requires – are virtually a living museum dating from the mid-nineteenth century. The shearing shed in particular is fascinating, constructed from termite-resistant native pine trunks sunk vertically in the ground and roofed with English iron, which was often carried in ships' holds as ballast. Inside there are some outstanding examples of bush carpentry, the handrails silky smooth from the years of rubbing with shearers' hands coated with lanolin from the sheep fleeces.

Angorichina will leave you with powerful memories, whether it's sharing a glass of champagne while watching the sunset or helping Ian wrestle his aircraft out of the hangar. Among their many qualities, Di and Ian practise the bush tradition of hospitality to perfection. Together, they will open your eyes to a side of Australia beyond your wildest imagination.

Angorichina exemplifies style
in food and accommodation
in the real outback.

IN STARK CONTRAST to the sunburned ranges
that surround it, Angorichina Station is a green
oasis of roses and lavender hedges surrounded
by green lawns and shady trees and even a
tennis court.

The homestead itself is a classic – a solid
stone building with thick walls to blunt the heat.
The original section of the homestead dates from
the 1860s, when pioneering graziers first drove
their flocks into the Flinders Ranges.

Step inside and you're instantly in another
world of music, flowers, books, antique
furnishings and paintings. Angorichina has just
two guest rooms, one at the front of the house,
with a private entrance off the verandah – a large
suite with subdued décor in a crisp, modern
style. The other guest room is located in the

former schoolhouse, a brick building set in
gardens just slightly apart from the homestead,
and prettily decorated in yellow tones reminiscent
of provincial France. Both guest suites have
private bathrooms.

Di is an accomplished cook who brings the
same sense of style to the dinner table that she
does to her house. In fact, sharing meals with Di
and Ian will be one of the highlights of your stay
at Angorichina. Dinners especially tend to be
long, and slightly riotous.

Both Ian and Di are great storytellers with a
rich fund of hilarious stories gathered from a
lifetime of living in the bush. Lunch is often
cooked on the barbeque among the pine trees
alongside the creek, a lovely place to spend a
couple of hours in the afternoon.

Beautiful fittings, attention to detail and a genuine affinity with bush life pervade the experience offered by the Farghers.

The vastness of the Flinders Ranges is at your doorstep on Angorichina, and learning from those with first hand knowledge of its secrets and wildlife is part of the joy of staying there.

A plethora of natural wonders and organised activities.

THERE'S HEAPS TO do here! Whether it's wildlife, photography, history or Aboriginal art and culture, the Flinders Ranges are among Australia's most invigorating and fascinating regions. One of the highlights is a visit to Chambers Gorge, where a creek seeps through a boulder-strewn bed, creating reed-lined pools at the foot of soaring peaks. In an arm of the gorge is one of the finest rock art sites in the Flinders Ranges, an entire wall of polished sandstone inscribed with circles and dots.

The guide on these expeditions is usually Arthur Coulthard, a ranger at adjacent Flinders Ranges National Park. Arthur is also a member of the local Adnyamathanha people, and his infectious enthusiasm as well as his knowledge of the plants, animals and Aboriginal rock art will animate your journey.

At least once during your stay, Ian will usher you into his plush Toyota four-wheel-drive and bounce you up to one of the high peaks around the property to watch the sunset with drinks and hors d'oeuvres. This is a moment of pure magic – watching the hills glow like embers in the warm evening light until finally the fire gives way to the night. This is also a time when the wildlife becomes active, and the hills are suddenly alive with wallabies, emus and kangaroos.

There is also the strong likelihood of a flight. Ian is an keen and vastly experienced pilot, one of the best stick and rudder men around, as anyone in this part of the world will tell you, and although the bumpy, rutted track that passes for his airstrip might not inspire confidence, this is not an opportunity to be missed. If you want to make sense of this vast country, you need to see it from the air. At 3000 feet, the landscape that seems anarchic and random at ground level suddenly becomes as regular as waves on the ocean. Layers of ancient sandstones that have been shoved high into the air by colliding tectonic plates form cogent patterns, each layer a separate band of sediment that was laid down when this was a vast sea bed.

The scenery is amazing, and includes such wonders as Wilpena Pound, photographers' favourite of the Flinders Ranges.

ANGORICHINA STATION

LOCATION: 510 kilometres north of Adelaide.

GETTING THERE: Best access is via light aircraft from Adelaide. Driving time is about six hours.

WHAT'S INCLUDED: All meals, drinks and activities.

MAKING THE MOST OF IT: The summer months between November and February often see temperatures rise above 36 degrees Celsius. The rest of the year is more comfortable, and even mid-winter days are typically mild and sunny. Rugged footwear and sun protection are a must at any time of the year.

CONTACT: Outback Encounter
33 Queen Street, Thebarton
South Australia, 5031, Australia
Telephone + 61 8 **8354 4405**
Facsimile + 61 8 **8354 4406**
Email info@outbackencounter.com
Website www.outbackencounter.com

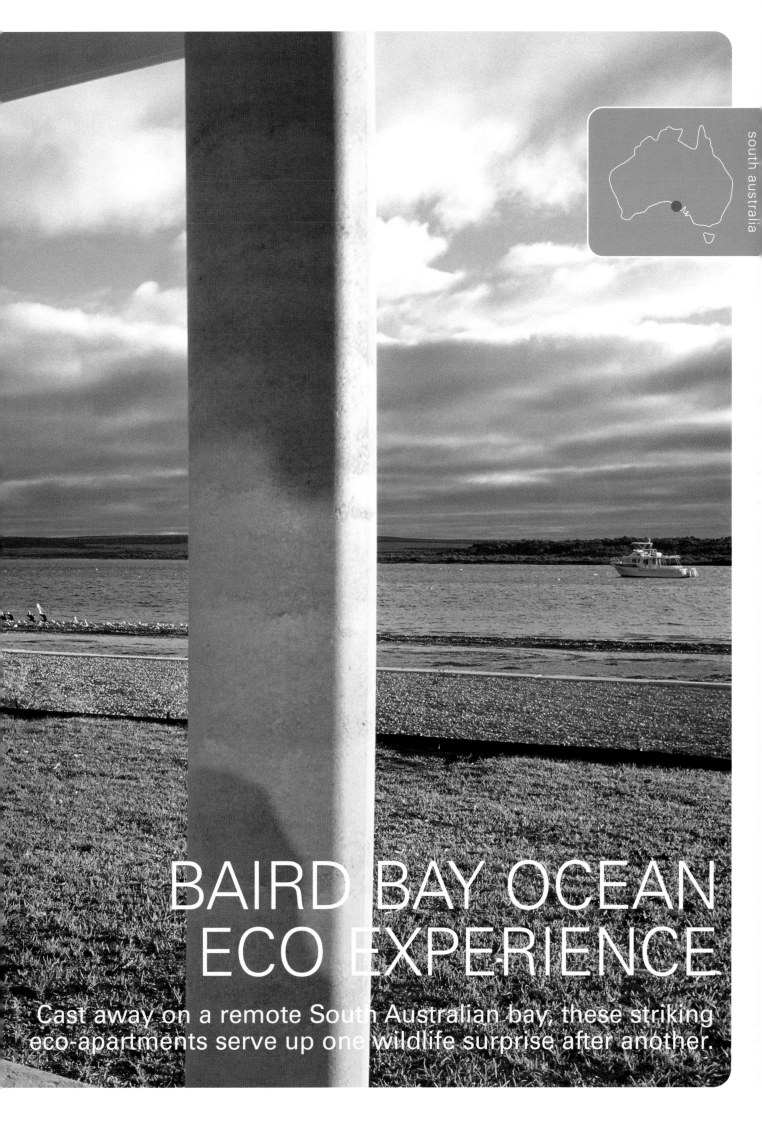

BAIRD BAY OCEAN ECO EXPERIENCE

Cast away on a remote South Australian bay, these striking eco-apartments serve up one wildlife surprise after another.

Bilbies, pelicans and sea lions provide the spectacle, while the apartments offer the creature comforts. Trish (feeding the pelicans) and Alan Payne are closely tuned into the creatures and moods of the bay and delight in sharing their knowledge with guests.

The siren song of Baird Bay is the music that drew Alan and Trish Payne to this remarkable place.

WHEN YOU CRUISE down the Flinders Highway along the west coast of South Australia's Eyre Peninsula, it's easy to overlook the turnoff to Baird Bay. Even if you take the gravel road that wanders through the sheep paddocks, you might wonder if the big bay that opens at your feet is worth the drive. But if you've been paying attention, you might have noticed that there seems to be an extraordinary number of birds wheeling in the sky overhead. Some 200 species have been recorded in the vicinity of Baird Bay. Many are sea birds – the promise of an exceptional marine environment.

Alan and Trish Payne were typical of the travellers with time on their hands and no particular place to go who happened to turn off the highway one day and head for Baird Bay; they found far more than they'd bargained for. "We just came because we were told the fishing was good," Alan says. And it was, and so it remains. What they didn't expect though, was Jones Island. Sitting smack in the middle of the channel guarding the approaches to the bay, Jones Island hosts Australia's only mainland breeding colony of sea lions. "We couldn't believe it," says Trish. "They'd swim right up to the boat, look us over and wave their front flippers around as if they were inviting us in for a swim. So we slipped into the water and the bond has been growing stronger ever since."

There was more. In the deeper waters of the main channel was a pod of bottlenose dolphins that seemed enchanted by the company of humans, and prepared to interact. Overhead was a big sky filled with drifting pelicans, and at sunset the bay turned to liquid gold. Within a couple of days of arriving they'd bought land on the edge of the bay, and this has been their home ever since.

The experience has turned them into fervent conservationists with a deep and passionate affection for their coastal home and all the creatures that live there – and one that they are only too happy to share with visitors. They know the history and the relationships of many of the animals that live here, and just sharing their enthusiasm and hearing their stories is an inspiration.

However, Baird Bay is not for everyone. It's a long drive from the nearest airport at Ceduna, and the human presence is barely a scratch on the landscape. Although it's comfortable, sophisticated it's not. Baird Bay – population three – is not the sort of township to set hearts fluttering. But this is a place of quiet magnificence mixed with moments of wild exuberance, such as when you plunge into the sea with a playful sea lion that explodes from the water just a couple of metres away. Baird Bay offers a remarkable experience, and only time and patience are required to unlock its secrets.

Here you will be spoiled in a palatial apartment equipped in a glowing, contemporary style.

SET AT THE back of the beach, surrounded by green lawns that are a favourite grazing ground for the local wallabies, Alan and Trish have built two striking contemporary lodges that stand out dramatically against the natural bushland.

The lodges have been built from rammed earth, which creates an adobe-like, textured finish with superior insulation properties, ensuring the lodges stay cool throughout the summer, and to absorb the warmth of the winter sun. Inside, the lodges are extremely spacious, comfortably furnished and comprehensively equipped. In the larger of the two lodges, the kitchen has a gleaming Miele espresso machine built into the wall, which produces masterful coffee at the press of a button. Big glass doors slide open to a view of beach, sky, sea and pelicans standing along the foreshore. Between the two lodges is a large barbeque area with a 12-seat table.

All meals are provided by a local chef, John Buckley, also a keen fisherman who can often be seen out in his boat on the bay when he's not occupied in the kitchen. John's skill is especially evident in the refinement and delicacy that he brings to the regional seafood. The local Coffin Bay oysters are a legend throughout Australia, known for their plumpness and their silky texture, while the tuna is exported direct to Japan where it commands a high price – and these are just two of the many outstanding foods found in this part of the world. Seafood lovers are in for a real treat! ➘

Rammed earth walls insulate the beautiful rooms and frame postcard views of the bay, which is home to abundant wildlife and exceptional seafood.

Frisky, agile and sociable, anytime is playtime for the sea lions of Baird Bay, while sunsets are a gift from the heavens.

IT'S ALL ABOUT the sea, and the headline event is swimming with the sea lions off Jones Island. Sea lions are the chimpanzees of the sea – fast, agile and playful – and they thrive on interaction with humans. Apart from the Galapagos Islands, this is the only place on Earth where you can swim with wild sea lions. Be prepared though – the sea is often chilly even in the wetsuits that Alan and Trish provide, the current can be strong despite the relative shelter of the pool where most of the sea lion encounters take place and there are no guarantees that the animals will interact. "It's completely up to them," says Trish. "We don't feed them and we don't land on the beach or go near them when they're resting. These are wild animals and they set the level of interaction." However, judging from the way they steam out from the shore when the boat arrives, there seems little risk that they will ever get bored with human company.

Slip into the chest-deep water and the sea lions will approach, making tumble turns just centimetres from your nose. Stay long enough and if the animals decide you're sociable company and they may even tickle your feet with their bristly whiskers.

After the sea lion encounter, the boat pulls into deeper water where you can swim with the resident dolphins. Powerful and lightning fast, these animals often come so close that you can hear their high-pitched chatter. The vessel Alan and Trish use for these trips is the *Investigator*, a 12-metre monohull that was purpose-built for these waters, with a broad stern deck that is also ideal for fishing trips in the turbulent waters of the Southern Ocean.

About a one-hour drive south-east along the coast in Venus Bay Conservation Park, two small Australian native species – bettongs and bilbies – have been reintroduced to an area that has been fenced to exclude feral animals such as foxes and cats, and the result is extraordinary, a teeming population within the space of a few years.

These animals are nocturnal and a tour of the Conservation Park with Alan will reveal an astonishing abundance of both species, a dramatic illustration of the impact that feral species have had on the native animal population.

At Baird Bay, the animal kingdom will remind you just you how good it feels to be alive.

BAIRD BAY OCEAN ECO EXPERIENCE

LOCATION: 745 kilometres north-west of Adelaide. From Ceduna Airport, it's a two-hour drive.

GETTING THERE: Fly from Adelaide to Ceduna, then drive.

WHAT'S INCLUDED: All meals and activities.

MAKING THE MOST OF IT: An underwater camera is a great asset. The best footwear is all-terrain sandals that are at home on the beach, in the water and on the boat. Wetsuits are provided, but take maximum sun protection.

CONTACT: Outback Encounter
33 Queen Street Thebarton,
South Australia, 5031 Australia
Telephone: + 61-8-8354 4405
Facsimile: + 61-8-8354 4406
Email: info@outbackencounter.com
Website: www.outbackencounter.com

LIFETIME PRIVATE RETREATS

Three eclectic villas set in a glorious Kangaroo Island bay have lashings of Australian style.

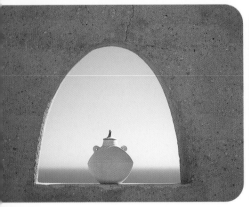

Sky House lives up to its name with sweeping panoramas, while the Mediterranean-inspired Cliff House is a bastion of good living and serenity.

We all need some soul food, and here on
Kangaroo Island you'll find it in abundance.

FROM THE TIME you step off the plane from
Adelaide, Kangaroo Island will astonish you.
Whether it's the wildlife, the plants or the
scenery, this is an island packed full of surprises,
and high on that list of surprises is Lifetime
Private Retreats.

Lifetime consists of three self-contained
houses dotted across a vast bowl of pastureland
on the north coast of the island. At the foot of the
bowl is Snellings Beach, a glorious sweep of
white sand, but as lovely as it is – and as
luxurious as the accommodation may be – the
experience transcends physical boundaries.
Lifetime brings a new concept to the
accommodation business, and not just on
Kangaroo Island, but the whole of Australia.

From the moment you arrive at your chosen
accommodation at Lifetime, you step into slightly
altered reality. From the whimsical décor to the
burning candles to the music on the sound
system, there's a touch of fantasy about it, an
urge to dress-up, make-believe and return to the
simplicities of childhood. The sensation continues
throughout your stay, with a series of small
delights calculated to catch you unawares and
bring you to slightly heightened awareness of this
special place.

Lifetime results from a coalition of the unusual
talents of the Hannaford family. Nick Hannaford is
the motivating force behind Hannaford's Special
Events, "Tailors of dreams and merchants of
magic", which has been choreographing events for
the corporate sector and visiting rock stars and
royalty for more than a decade. Nick Hannaford
was the inspiration behind *Flames of the Forest*
in North Queensland, a candlelit rainforest dining
experience incorporating elements of Aboriginal
culture. This is a fantasy evening with a
difference, and Nick has imported some of that
wizardry to Kangaroo Island.

Rachel Hannaford, Nick's sister, has a
background as a chef and a musician, and has
recently qualified as a yoga teacher. Their mother,
Belinda, who spent many years operating
restaurants in Adelaide, has made her family's
property at Snellings Beach her home for many
years now. During that time she has welcomed
many visitors to this secluded part of the island –
and crafted some very special experiences for
them – and it is her energy, her passion and her
flair that have made this a memorable place for
many Australians.

The Hannafords have never done things quite
by the rules, and their creativity is infectious. This
is a place to try something new, and surrendering
yourself to the talents of these energetic
personalities will bring a very different dimension
to your Kangaroo Island sojourn.

Far more than mere food and lodging, a stay at
Lifetime is an experience. Staying here feels
more like staying in the house of a gregarious and
worldly friend who happens to live in a glorious
and isolated location, keeps a fine wine cellar,
cooks like a wizard and makes inspired
conversation over the dinner table. This is a
journey for the soul.

The beach kiosk dresses up for dinner. You can take a barefoot walk on the sand, watch the sun melt into the sea and prepare for a feast.

Three very individual houses, combined with innovative cooking and plenty of panache.

LIFETIME CONSISTS OF three separate, self-contained houses, each totally different. Perched on the hillside overlooking Snellings Beach, Cliff House is a Mediterranean-inspired, three-bedroom villa with a big terrace at the front and a whimsical little turret, with a double-size circular bed that occupies the entire tower. At the top of the hill behind, Sky House is a romantic hideaway just for two, a Moroccan-inspired fantasy with rammed earth walls and a voluptuous, mostly red colour scheme accented with twinkling lights. The multi-purpose sitting room opens to a courtyard with wings on either side that reach out to embrace the wide-angle view at your feet. In one of those wings is the bedroom, which has a king-size bed and a gorgeous bathroom behind. Latest addition is Stone House, which also has three bedrooms, cloistered among the coastal woodland close to the beach.

All houses have everything you need for an indulgent escape, from a complete sound system to beach toys to a well-stocked larder – but then chances are you won't be doing too much cooking. Rachel Hannaford cut her chef's teeth working for a string of restaurants in London, Melbourne and Adelaide. Her CV also includes a highly unusual stint catering for the Dalai Lama and a dessert for Mick Jagger, which featured oversized chocolate lips. Mediterranean influences are dominant in her cooking, but the food that she prepares for guests at Lifetime from breakfast to dinner moves easily among a wide repertoire of cuisines, Asian and Middle Eastern as well as European. However, as much as the innovative and passionate food that she serves, it's where and how she serves it that makes meals at Lifetime special.

Among the possible venues for her evening feasts is a century-old shearing shed furnished with couches draped with sparkly sequined fabrics and candelabras, a bower within the limbs of an ancient fig tree that is lit with fairy lights and candles and a beach shelter, which is pure magic on summer evenings, when a fire burns on the sand in front.

Interiors are luxurious, and packed with intriguing details. Even the tub in the Sky House has a view made in heaven.

OUTBACK ENCOUNTER PORTFOLIO
MEMBER

Take your pick of tours, wildlife … or even yoga.

MOST OF KANGAROO Island's headline attractions are located on the south coast, and while these are within easy reach of Lifetime, the north coast has a charm all its own.

Snellings Beach is one of the island's loveliest, a sheltered sweep of sand bracketed by rocky headlands at either end. Even at the height of summer, half-a-dozen people constitute a crowd here. Kangaroo Island offers every inducement to move. It has wildlife wonders that you won't see easily in any other part of the country, a wild, wind-flayed coastline, forests and coastal heaths of subtle beauty and some fascinating characters who make this their home.

Whatever your inclinations, Lifetime can arrange a tour with Adventure Charters, the leading tour operator on the island. These are potent attractions, and it would be a grave oversight to miss them. But Lifetime is itself a special experience, and you should plan to spend time relaxing, on the terraces, on the beach and enjoying the luxurious sense of idleness that the houses foster.

Guided yoga and meditation are other options. Rachel is a yoga teacher, trained at the Baron Baptiste Vinyasa Yoga Institute in Hawaii. "It's great because there are no levels in Baron Baptiste Yoga, so it's suitable for everyone from beginners to advanced. It's a very dynamic, very vigorous form of yoga," says Rachel, who also organises yoga retreats for small groups. In these wild and natural surroundings, a private class with Rachel is something to treasure.

SOUTH
AUSTRALIA

ADELAIDE

Yorke
Peninsula

**LIFETIME PRIVATE
RETREATS**

Snellings
Beach

Cape Jervis   Fleurieu
Peninsula

Kingscote

Playford   Penneshaw

Flinders Chase   Highway
National Park   KANGAROO
ISLAND

Cape Gantheaume
National Park

LIFETIME PRIVATE RETREATS

LOCATION: On the north coast of Kangaroo Island, about 45 minutes drive from Kingscote.

GETTING THERE: REX and Emu Airways operate several flights daily between Adelaide and Kingscote. Sealink ferries make up to 12 crossings between Cape Jervis and Penneshaw a day.

WHAT'S INCLUDED: All meals, drinks and road transfers from Kingscote Airport.

MAKING THE MOST OF IT: Be prepared for cool weather at any time of the year. The baggage allowance on flights to the island is 13kg with Emu, and 15kg with REX, excess baggage can usually be brought over on a later flight.

CONTACT: Outback Encounter
33 Queen Street, Thebarton
South Australia, 5031, Australia
Telephone + 61 8 **8354 4405**
Facsimile + 61 8 **8354 4406**
Email info@outbackencounter.com
Website www.outbackencounter.com

ODYSSEY RIVER CRUISES

Cruising the Murray River is one of Australia's great adventures. Here's how to do it in style.

The *Odyssey* offers an entrée to this glorious world, under the able direction of Captain Des Eiffe and first mate Annette Eiffe.

Mostly the Murray is an empty brown road that ignites at sunset.

THE MURRAY IS Australia's second-longest river and one of the world's great waterways, with a total length close to 2530 kilometres. In its wandering journey from the alpine country on the border between New South Wales and Victoria until it meets the ocean south-east of Adelaide, the Murray is a constantly unfolding drama, with a new chapter at every turn.

A cruise between its banks is one of the greatest journeys Australia has to offer, combining history, romance, scenery, wildlife and adventure, and the best way to see it is with a cruise aboard the *Odyssey*. While there are plenty of houseboats you can hire for a do-it-yourself journey, the Odyssey is the only vessel on the river that combines the essential qualities of luxury and refinement and a high level of personal service in a small-scale package. This is the only small cruiser that you can rent out yourself for an indulgent voyage that comes complete with a captain, crew and chef. All you have to do is sit back, relax, enjoy and let someone else worry about the ropes.

From her base at Mannum, just over a one-hour drive from Adelaide, the *Odyssey* offers a number of different river cruise itineraries, from three-day trips for individual travellers to one-week voyages that take you through the river locks to the town of Loxton. It's also possible to tailor-make an itinerary to suit your own requirements, and while a voyage aboard the

Odyssey is fun for just two, it's even better if you can put together a small group of like-minded sybarites.

The Murray plays a proud part in Australia's history. Since time immemorial it has been an important resource for the Aboriginal people, for whom it was a provided food as well as shelter in the rocky cliffs along its banks. During the late 19th century the river was a major artery for trade to and from the interior. Paddle steamers towed barges laden with cargoes of wool and wheat from new settlements that had been carved out along the river, and a whole industry grew up to service this trade, from the timber-cutters who supplied them with fuel for their steam engines to the rivermen who worked the locks. The expansion of the railways brought an end to that colourful era, and these days the river is a sleepy, slow-moving giant, gurgling through quiet backwaters and country towns where every creaking door has a story to tell.

The scenery along the river alternates from river gums that crowd massively at the water's edge to stark red cliffs. Large towns are few. Most of the scattered settlements consist of just a few houses. Sometimes there are other vessels, but for the most part the river is an empty brown road that ignites at sunset. For anyone with the power to wonder, the journey aboard the *Odyssey* will put wings on your imagination. ↘

Delicious food, cooked to order, adds to the experience.

THE *ODYSSEY* HAS four handsome staterooms, two on either side of the vessel, each with a zip-apart king-size bed and TV monitors and reading lamps as well as plenty of storage space. Each stateroom has its own neat and well-equipped ensuite bathroom. On the top deck there's a large lounge with big sofas for long, lazy afternoons, a bar and a dining area. To one side of the lounge is a separate bathroom with a huge spa bath.

Three times a day, your river journey will be interrupted by the delicious smells wafting from the galley at the stern of the vessel. Food is an important part of the voyage aboard the *Odyssey*. Breakfast might begin with a selection of cereals, a fruit compote and yoghurt with a selection of fresh fruit juices followed by poached eggs and bacon with tea or coffee. For lunch, options may include a warm seafood salad, or perhaps a Thai-style chicken with jasmine rice.

Dinner might begin with an entrée of oysters or smoked salmon, followed by a chargrilled beef tenderloin with a port wine and pepper demi-glace, or perhaps a roast rack of lamb with a lime glaze – a feast for the taste buds celebrated with some of South Australia's finest wines. All meals are prepared by a chef – which means you can have your meals cooked to order, and each mealtime will bring fresh surprises.

The *Odyssey* ties up under huge river red gums and sets you ashore at a fascinating Aboriginal cultural site upstream from Walkers Flat and a spotlight tour to view wallabies and wombats after dark. And there's always plenty of time for fishing.

Wildlife galore, Aboriginal culture … and a glimpse of the famous Barossa Valley.

ALTHOUGH SIMPLY DRIFTING between the Murray's banks has a charm all its own, several times a day the *Odyssey* will tie up at the huge river red gums and send you ashore for a journey of discovery – and there is much to enjoy.

At Ngaut Ngaut, an Aboriginal site upstream from Walkers Flat, the sandstone wall is notched with petroglyphs of animals and totemic designs from the time when this was an important habitation site for the Nganguraku people. The Nganguraku still maintain their powerful spiritual connection with the river, and with a trained guide, you can clearly see depicted in these walls a record of changing life along the Murray – including the time when freshwater dolphins once inhabited this part of the river.

Further upstream, David LeBrun operates Big Bend by Night, a spotlight tour in an open-topped wagon to view wallabies and wombats, which are usually present in their hundreds at Sunnydale Station, his Murray River farm. The river is dotted with history – towns and museums and restored paddleboats along the riverbank. At several places the Murray passes close to South Australia's vineyards, including the famous Barossa Valley, which has some of the prettiest scenery as well as the most illustrious architecture of any winegrowing region in the country. A day tour of the area can be easily arranged from the *Odyssey* – or perhaps a round of golf if you'd prefer.

The wildlife along the river is dazzling. You'll certainly see pelicans and black swans, and probably also kangaroos and wallabies, sulphur-crested cockatoos and goannas. At many places the river floods into quiet backwaters where wading birds stalk along the reedy water margins.

ODYSSEY RIVER CRUISES

LOCATION: *Odyssey*'s home port of Mannum is 84 kilometres east of Adelaide, about a one-hour drive.

GETTING THERE: Transfers are available from Adelaide.

WHAT'S INCLUDED: All meals, drinks and activities

MAKING THE MOST OF IT: Take casual clothing, a hat, walking shoes and some good books for long, lazy afternoons.

CONTACT: Outback Encounter
33 Queen Street, Thebarton
South Australia, 5031, Australia
Telephone + 61 8 **8354 4405**
Facsimile + 61 8 **8354 4406**
Email info@outbackencounter.com
Website www.outbackencounter.com

PRAIRIE HOTEL

Against a blazing sky, the Prairie reworks the iconic outback pub and infuses it with a quirky sense of humour and style.

A new kind of outback experience, delivered with panache, intelligence and a ripping good time.

OUTBACK AUSTRALIA IS known for its quirky take on life, but even by these exaggerated standards of eccentricity, the sign that announces the Prairie Hotel comes as a surprise. "On Your Plate – 3km" it reads, beneath a trio of yellow road signs that depict an emu, a kangaroo and a camel in silhouette. And they're not kidding.

Turn off the highway from Port Augusta to Leigh Creek at the town of Parachilna and you're in for another surprise. Although the façade of the hotel looks like something out of the pioneering past, grafted onto the rear is a soaring, contemporary wing that makes dramatic use of glass, steel and corrugated iron.

Step through the door and you're in a crowded front bar with all the essential bush-pub elements, but it is in the adjoining dining room that the Prairie reveals its true colours. The décor is unusual, to say the least. Set among rustic tables that bear the scars and dents of decades

of use, there's a bunch of 'flowers' made from tin cans, the edges of which have been peeled back to make petals; a picture frame decorated with a punctured football; a pair of well-worn riding boots and a cricket bat; ancient fuel panniers, and abstract constructions made from rabbit traps and bits of an old whip.

Its position is exceptional. Surrounded by rippling red sand hills, salt lakes, abandoned stone cottages and the seared, serrated majesty of the Flinders Ranges, the Prairie has become a favourite for commercial makers in search of instant outback verité for the latest four-wheel-drive ad. Even Hollywood puts in an occasional appearance, and scenes from *Rabbit Proof Fence* and *Holy Smoke!* starring Harvey Keitel and Kate Winslet were shot here. This makes for some fascinating encounters. Sitting in the bar, the person at the next stool could be a ringer from one of the local stations, a backpacker, an

Order a beer, and get ready for the sunset to paint the sky. After that, treat yourself to some of the local produce, as advertised on the way to the hotel that is a labour of love for Jane and Ross Fargher, who are normally seen on the other side of the bar.

eminent landscape painter or an impresario scouting locations for the next edition of *Opera in the Outback*.

The creative force behind the hotel is Jane Fargher. Jane arrived here when she married Ross Fargher, one of the fourth generation of Farghers to own grazing properties in the Flinders Ranges. When the Prairie Hotel came up for sale in 1991, Jane saw the potential and seized the opportunity to create outback accommodation with fine food and a style and personality all its own. And all this has been achieved without once descending to cliché. There are no tricked-up outdoor toilets, no antiquated automobiles stuck on the roof, and apart from the occasional misguided visitor, no hats with dangling corks in the bar.

The Prairie represents a new kind of outback experience – served with panache, intelligence and a devilish sense of humour.

Traditional materials are given new life with contemporary design at the Prairie Hotel, where an eclectic mix of feral food is served with humour and style and the standard of accommodation belies the remote location.

Irresistible food and a quality, somewhat quirky twist to outback life.

ALTHOUGH IT MIGHT look fairly innocuous at first glance, the handsome, historic stone hotel is a trailblazer that has pioneered a whole new style of food and accommodation in outback Australia. In the process, the Prairie has put the Flinders Ranges on the wish list for a different kind of traveller. Beneath a stuffed animal head mounted on the wall, the menu lists feral antipasto, quandong pie and the house specialty, the feral mixed grill, abbreviated to FMG – kangaroo fillet, camel sausage, goat chop and emu pâté.

Although the menu makes much of bush tucker of the four-legged kind – and jokes about road kill flow with boom-boom regularity in the dining room – the trade in feral animals is strictly controlled. Even though they are hunted in this

area, kangaroo and wild goat are sent to Adelaide for processing and inspection before they appear on the dinner table at the Prairie.

Rooms at the Prairie come in two distinct styles. Located at the back of the original pub, Heritage Rooms are neat, spacious and recently renovated. Further back, in the modern extension, Deluxe Rooms are larger still, each with its own ensuite bathroom. Top of the range are the Executive Rooms, which come with double-size spa baths and two queen-size beds. All rooms in this new wing are sunk waist-deep into the ground to take advantage of the natural insulation that the earth provides, although air conditioning is needed to tone down the Flinders' withering midsummer heat.

The evening lightshow draws a crowd, while there's frosty consolation on tap for those inside. A night at the Prairie will light a blaze in the heart, all you have to do is follow the arrow to this grazing ground with a difference.

A favourite with photographers, painters and filmmakers in search of outback scenery.

LOCATED ON THE broad plains just to the west of the Flinders Ranges, the Prairie Hotel makes an ideal base for exploring one of the most sensational parts of outback Australia. Here, surrounded by the arid wasteland of the great salt lakes, the ancient bed of a great sea has been sculpted by millions of years of rain and sun into a fractured, furrowed landscape of deep valleys covered with casuarinas and cypress pines which fall into creeks lined with river red gums. For wildlife watching, bushwalking, photography, Aboriginal rock art or just soaking up the sights and sounds of outback Australia, the Flinders are in a class apart.

One of the best ways to see this country is from the air, and the Skysafari helicopter which is based at Parachilna can whisk you away on a tour of the surroundings, which can be anything from a hilltop sunset tour to an overflight of Lake Torrens or Wilpena Pound. Four-wheel-drive tours are another option, and tours can be arranged from the hotel.

Don't miss Brachina Gorge, the most inspiring of all the roads that cross the Central Flinders Ranges. If time allows, take the road that turns north off this road along the Aroona Valley, in the shadow of the Heysen Range, which takes its name from one of South Australia's most illustrious landscape painters. The road ends at a spring where the vestiges of the Aroona Station lie crumbling and toppled amid the grasslands. This is a never-fail place to see wallabies, and usually a few emus. A number of bushwalks begin from here.

PRAIRIE HOTEL

LOCATION: 470 kilometres north of Adelaide.

GETTING THERE: Combine the Prairie with a flying visit to Angorichina (pp 16-23), or drive from Adelaide.

WHAT'S INCLUDED: Breakfast.

MAKING THE MOST OF IT: March to late October is the ideal time for touring in the Flinders. Take clothing and footwear that doesn't blanch at dust and rocks, and a hat – preferably broad-brimmed – and sun block are essential.

CONTACT: Outback Encounter
33 Queen Street Thebarton,
South Australia, 5031 Australia
Telephone: + 61-8-**8354 4405**
Facsimile: + 61-8-**8354 4406**
Email: info@outbackencounter.com
Website: www.outbackencounter.com

OUTBACK ENCOUNTER PORTFOLIO
MEMBER

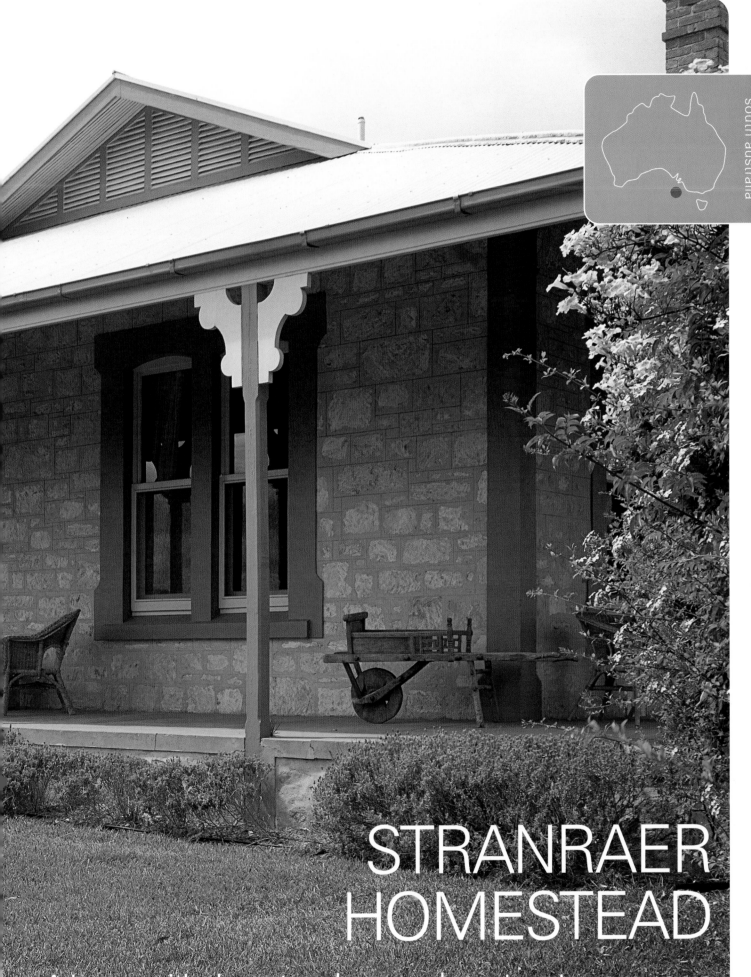

STRANRAER HOMESTEAD

A house with character, charm and great gastronomy on a sprawling sheep property on majestic Kangaroo Island.

In their handsome country home, Graham and Lyn Wheaton maintain the traditions that were laid down by their ancestors a century ago.

A strong sense of tradition, and a welcome as wide as a country mile greets you at Stranraer.

KANGAROO ISLAND IS one of Australia's rustic wonders, a treasure chest brimming with wildlife and wild sensations, and Stranraer is the perfect base from which to explore this amazing island.

Perched on a rise at the end of an avenue of stately pine trees surrounded by sheep pastures, Stranraer comes straight from the classic Australian country mould. Constructed from pale blocks of local limestone that were quarried and brought to the site by horse dray in the 1920s, the handsome homestead has been immaculately restored by its owners, Graham and Lyn Wheaton. Climb the steps to the broad, shady verandah, open the front door and you're in a wide corridor that runs toward the kitchen and dining room at the rear of the house. The detail is lavish – from the leadlight panels in the front door to the fireplaces to the ornate moulded ceilings to the antiques, the brocade curtains and the collection of oilskin jackets hanging on pegs that suggest a brisk sense of purpose.

High among Stranraer's attributes are Graham and Lyn themselves, the perfect hosts, with a welcome as wide as a country mile, and both quietly in love with their island home. The guest book is filled with tributes to their hospitality, their house, their knowledge – and most of all, to

the food that they serve. They might subtitle their accommodation "bed and breakfast", yet the bare-bones tag hardly does justice to the feasts that appear at Lyn and Graham's table.

A typical day at Stranraer begins with a generous country breakfast, after which guests are collected by their tour hosts to spend the day out strolling among the seals, watching the birds or counting koalas, returning toward evening with plenty of time to relax before dinner. The homestead is about a 20-minute drive from Kingscote, an ideal central location that puts it within comfortable reach of some of the major attractions, which are widely dispersed across the island.

While Kangaroo Island will deliver all the wildlife and wilderness that the tourist brochures promise, Stranraer brings another dimension to the experience – character, sophistication and a taste for the finer things in life that is totally unexpected in this wild and majestic kingdom. Better still, it comes at a bargain price that seems to come from another era. If you're looking for small, distinctive accommodation with wonderful food, fine surroundings and a generous dose of style, nowhere else on Kangaroo Island even comes close.

In décor and furnishings, Stranraer revels in the opulence and ornament of the Victorian era, while Lyn's cuisine is a more modern wonder.

Treats everywhere for lovers of country life ...
and fresh, home-cooked food to die for.

STRANRAER'S FOUR GUEST rooms are arranged of either side of the broad T-shaped corridor that runs from the front door to the kitchen. All the guest rooms are large, but rather than altering their character to create ensuite bathrooms, only one bedroom has its own ensuite bathroom. Another has a private adjoining bathroom and two more share a large central bathroom. Rooms are decorated and furnished in a warm, romantic style that harks back to the Victorian era, with well-polished antique furnishings and an opulent, romantic colour scheme.

Although dinners are optional, most guests choose to dine in – and with good reason. Lyn is a self-taught cook, but also a highly sophisticated one who lists teaching cooking in local schools among her host of achievements.

"I love fresh food, and I love things to taste like what they are," says Lyn, who takes her inspiration from a wide array of sources. "I adapt, I take people's ideas from books and magazines

and I work out what I can do with it," adds Lyn, a staunch advocate for such local products as sheep's milk ricotta, free-range eggs, olive oil, smoked trout and the excellent Kangaroo Island seafood, including crayfish, mussels and marron, and the herbs and fruit fresh from her own garden. So successful is the result that Lyn is frequently asked for her recipes. So frequently, in fact, that she's published a book of full of the best of them, complete with illustrations by a local artist. "I just got tired of writing the recipes out for people, it seemed the logical thing to do," laughs Lyn as she stands in her kitchen, the source of the delicious smells that waft through the house.

Breakfasts are marvellous – cereals, fruit, juices, coffee, toast and a cooked dish – which might be poached eggs served with ham and fresh hollandaise. "To me, breakfast is just the worst looking meal in most hotels. They just don't come up with anything different," says Lyn, whose breakfasts never fail to delight and surprise.

From the windmills to the shearing shed to the outbuildings and the dogs, Stranraer is the perfect place to experience life on a working sheep station.

Inspiration, and a wind that sings in the pastures.

ALTHOUGH MOST GUESTS choose to spend their days exploring the natural wonders of Kangaroo Island, Stranraer has marvels of its own. A 15-minute stroll across the sheep pastures on the north-western side of the house will take you to a line of low hills and a tangled woodland beyond that encloses a huge, shallow lagoon that provides a roost for many thousands of water birds.

Stranraer is a 1290-hectare sheep property, and there is nowhere better to get a close-up look at life and work on a sheep station. The shearing shed and the yards in the paddock are models of sturdy practicality, many built at the same time as the house. Show the slightest interest in sheep and Graham will whisk you off on a tour of the property that he now operates with his son, Jason.

The walled garden is a treasury of small delights, from the lavender hedge that surrounds the house to the nectarine tree at the side and the cottage garden, planted with roses and plumbago.

In the hollow just below the house, the MacGillivray Cricket Club is a tribute to the passion of Robert Wheaton, Graham's grandfather. The ground is still scrupulously maintained, and well used during the summer cricket season, when you might happen to catch a game in progress.

STRANRAER HOMESTEAD

LOCATION: 30 kilometres south of Kingscote, which is 120km south-west of Adelaide.

GETTING THERE: Emu Airways operates several flights daily between Adelaide and Kingscote, the main town on Kangaroo Island. Flight time is about 30 minutes. Sealink ferries make up to 12 45-minute crossings between Cape Jervis and Penneshaw each day.

WHAT'S INCLUDED: Breakfast. Three-course dinners are available by arrangement.

MAKING THE MOST OF IT: Dress casual, but be prepared for cool and windy weather at any time of the year. Internet access and ATM machines are available in Kingscote.

CONTACT: Outback Encounter
33 Queen Street Thebarton,
South Australia, 5031, Australia
Telephone + 61 8 **8354 4405**
Facsimile + 61 8 **8354 4406**
Email info@outbackencounter.com
Website www.outbackencounter.com

EL QUESTRO
HOMESTEAD

The spectacular Cockburn Ranges provide the perfect backdrop to this beautifully-appointed homestead.

Luxurious surroundings and fine food provide a perfect base for experiencing the untamed wonders and wildlife of the Kimberley region.

JUST AS YOU'RE dressing for the cocktails that are an evening ritual at El Questro Homestead, look out into the depths of the gorge just below your room and there's bound to be a couple of crocodiles floating on the surface. They are always there for the bread which the staff throw into the water. Not that crocodiles are fond of bread, but the bread attracts fish, and fish attract crocodiles. They remind you that despite the velvet glove, El Questro is still part of the wild frontier. For anyone who prefers their wilderness served with a full complement of luxury trimmings, the Homestead rooms at El Questro are as good as it gets.

The homestead's setting is simply superb. Amid a cool oasis shaded by palm trees and tropical greenery, it sits on a rise, perched on rock walls that plummet into the Chamberlain River. At the heart of the homestead is a spacious, open-plan room decorated with Asian furnishings and cooled by ceiling fans. Under the verandahs are cane couches and shady spots for idle afternoons. Surrounded by lawns that slope down toward the deep trough of the Chamberlain Gorge, the homestead's swimming pool scatters threads of golden sunlight across its surface. On the far side of the river, the ground rises to the heights of the Cockburn Ranges which glow in the light of the setting sun as if lit by an inner fire, casting a mirror image across the still, dark waters of the river.

You could sit here happily for hours just watching the birds that skim across the river and the changing patterns of light on the ranges, but

High above the gorge, you'll be enthralled by the views and the freshwater crocodiles far below.

El Questro comes with a full complement of activities, and the more you do, the more you'll enjoy the experience.

Located about a 90-minute drive from Kununurra, the town at the eastern gateway to the Kimberley, El Questro is a million-acre cattle station that has become a showcase for all the Kimberley has to offer – wildlife, red river gorges, waterholes – and much more besides. Its symbol is the boab, a tree from another planet. Bulbous, bloated, and bizarre, this African immigrant is an eccentric even by the exaggerated standards of Australia's taxonomy. According to the creation stories of Australia's Aborigines, the boab tree was planted upside-down in the earth as punishment for its pride and arrogance. During the dry season, when it loses its leaves, the boab looks like a tree from the kindergarten class, a ponderous, turnip-shaped trunk with a bunch of sticks waving madly at the sky. In old age – and a boab isn't old until its millennium – its bole might hollow out from lightning strikes, and the cavities inside ancient boabs have been used as homes, as stables and even as a prison cell.

Boabs dot the plains of El Questro, but the Kimberley is at its loveliest in its river gorges, and there are several delectable examples at El Questro, large rock pools where pandanus palms and paperbarks stroke the water lilies. Water brings life to this parched landscape, and there is no better place to watch for wildlife, dividing your time between the cool water and the warm rocks. ⬎

Fine dining, dazzling accommodation, luxury and style all around – the level of refinement at El Questro belies the raw wonders of the world at its doorstep.

Dinners are served outside under a blossoming night sky.

THE SIX GUEST rooms are located to one side of the homestead building, and each one is spacious, serene and luxuriously furnished. Each has a king-size bed, a private verandah and airconditioning as well as a full-size ensuite bathroom. The pick of the bunch are the three rooms that are perched right on the very brink of Chamberlain gorge. At the very top of the luxury ladder is the opulent Chamberlain Suite. Furnishings in the guest rooms are the same blend of Oriental pieces that are found throughout the rest of the house.

Meals are cooked by the homestead's chef, and the food is absolutely sensational. Three times a day you will be served with stylish, inventive cuisine that blends Asian and Mediterranean flavours with the very finest, freshest produce. All food, wines and drinks are included in the tariff. Dinners are served outside at a communal table on the deck, against a luscious backdrop of palm trees with the night sky blossoming overhead. Those who prefer can dine in privacy at a table on the edge of the cliff overlooking the gorge.

Whether it's seeking out Aboriginal rock art, throwing in a fishing line, swimming in a water hole or just watching the sunset, El Questro is a five-star experience.

ALTHOUGH IT MIGHT be hard to tear yourself away from the luxurious surrounds of the homestead, El Questro is also a springboard to one of the most sensational parts of the Kimberley. As an introduction to the million-acre property, a four-wheel-drive tour of the surroundings is a must. Some of the other options include hiking and trail riding on the station horses. There are electric-powered aluminium dinghies in which you can putter through the gorge below the homestead.

One of the loveliest trips takes you to Zebedee Springs, where you can luxuriate in the warm water surrounded by mossy rocks tat form a series of natural swimming pools. The springs are shaded by a canopy of livistonia palms, one of the few remnant stands of a species that once covered much of the continent when Australia was a much wetter place. The surrounding ranges also have some fine examples of Bradshaw art, the mysterious rock paintings that appear to be separate from the main body of Aboriginal rock art – and the creators of which are unknown to this day.

Another thrilling experience is a helicopter trip through the gorges, which are at their finest toward evening, when the red rock walls glow in the warm light. There's also the Mount Cockburn Safari – a two-day camping safari to experience the rugged grandeur of the Cockburn Ranges – with a luxury tent, guides and your own private chef in attendance.

Loll around on the lawn, bask by the pool –
or get among it all in Australia's rugged outback.

EL QUESTRO HOMESTEAD

LOCATION: About 100 kilometres west of Kununurra.

GETTING THERE: A 90-minute drive from Kununurra, or air transfer.

WHAT'S INCLUDED: All meals including beer and wine.

MAKING THE MOST OF IT: Expect heat and dust by day. Wear cool, loose clothing and sturdy walking shoes and a wide-brimmed hat, and be prepared to dress up for cocktails and dinner. The best time to visit is during the relatively cool months of the dry period which lasts from April to October, particularly the earlier part of that period.

CONTACT: Outback Encounter
33 Queen Street, Thebarton
South Australia, 5031, Australia
Telephone + 61 8 **8354 4405**
Facsimile + 61 8 **8354 4406**
Email info@outbackencounter.com
Website www.outbackencounter.com

THE BUSH CAMP
AT FARAWAY BAY

Isolated it may be, but that's part of the attraction.
You can't get more 'away from it all' and be so enchanted.

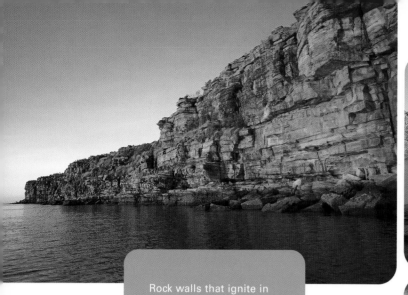

Rock walls that ignite in the evening light, beaches that are empty but for the occasional croc, brilliant views and a quiet place to relax – Bruce and Robyn Ellison preside over a place of miracles.

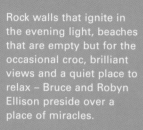

In a glorious setting on the Kimberley coast, you can just sit back and watch the wildlife swim by.

THE NAME SAYS it all. A one-hour flight north-west from Kununurra, the Bush Camp at Faraway Bay is set deep in the throat of a broad bay close to the northern tip of the Kimberley. The only way in is by plane or boat. So remote is the location that it didn't even have a name when Bruce Ellison came this way searching for a special place to build the lodge of his dreams. But to Bruce, Faraway Bay seemed an obvious choice.

It took some finding. A long-standing Kununurra resident, Bruce had spent years exploring the Kimberley coast by boat and helicopter, establishing camps for mining crews surveying the Kimberley for promising mineral sites. When Bruce found this place deep within the indentation that was to become Faraway Bay, he knew he'd found what he was looking for all along – a base from which to introduce visitors to the splendours of the Kimberley coast. It had an outstanding combination of factors – including a freshwater spring, relatively easy access by air, a stunning stretch of coastline, great fishing and proximity to the King George River, one of the natural wonders of the Kimberley.

The setting is glorious. From the camp's terrace, the hillside tumbles into the blue of the bay across a steep cliff studded with black rocks, yellow grasses and kapok trees. On either side the arms of the bay reach out to enfold the sea in arms that range in colour from charcoal to ochre.

The centrepiece of the camp is Eagle Lodge, an open-fronted structure with a slate floor, set in a commanding position overlooking the bay. This is the camp's restaurant, loungeroom and library. On the terrace below, the swimming pool twinkles in the sunlight. Just sitting here you could find plenty to fill in the day, relaxing in the hammock, lolling about in the plunge pool, watching the finches that come down to drink and scatter seed on their feeding table – and scattering themselves when a sea eagle descends to collect its breakfast of fish.

A favourite activity for guests is watching the wildlife swimming in the clear waters of the bay – dugongs, sharks and even crocodiles, which is another good reason to stick to the pool rather than to the sea. Another favourite is firing golf balls from the rock just below the lodge to the pin which lies on the beach below – Bruce's driving range.

But it's hard to sit still here. Sail out of the bay aboard one of Bruce's vessels and you'll be amazed at the scenery and the wildlife that awaits – a virtual National Geographic in three dimensions, just waiting to be discovered.

The accommodation at Faraway Bay doesn't try and compete with the glory of the surroundings, and the food always brings in the local wildlife for a closer look.

It's not all fishy, but if sea harvests take your fancy, go ahead and indulge.

FOOD AND LODGING at Faraway Bay challenges the 'bush' part of the name 'Bush Camp'. There are eight cabins set among the grass and rocks at the top of the slope, in red corrugated iron with screens all around that leave them open to the breeze and the shooshing night sounds of the waves. Each has fans and a small light, king-size beds that can be zipped apart and an outside shower at the front of the verandah. A central wet facility provides toilets and showers. It's some way short of deluxe, yet airconditioners and hair dryers in the rooms would strike a false note in these raw and awesome surroundings.

Food is one of the best things about Faraway Bay. Fish is a regular at the buffet-style meals – depending on what the fishermen have caught – and there's always a wide selection of leafy green salads, vegetable dishes and freshly-baked bread cooked by a chef who achieves small miracles in the open kitchen at the back of the dining room. For non-fish eaters there are always meat or vegetarian alternatives, and on excursions there's a picnic lunch with cool drinks.

Beer and wine are available for lunch and dinner, and there are all-day treats that emerge constantly from the kitchen – scones or muffins for morning and afternoon tea, and a never-ending supply of biscuits. A highlight is the dinners that are slow-cooked over the coals in the camp oven – which might be beef, lamb or chicken that falls apart in your mouth, saturated with rich flavours.

On, in or out of the water, there's a never-ending armada of things to do.

Learn how to cast a net for bait fish, admire the view, take a dip, take a cruise or practice your swing on a driving range with a difference – sunrise to sunset, there's something for every moment of the day.

OUTBACK
ENCOUNTER
PORTFOLIO
MEMBER

Map labels:
- Cape Londonderry
- Cape Talbot
- Kalumburu
- THE BUSH CAMP FARAWAY BAY
- TIMOR SEA
- Drysdale River National Park
- Oombulgurri Aboriginal Land
- Wyndham
- WESTERN AUSTRALIA
- Kununurra
- Gibb River Road

THE ACTIVITIES LIST at Faraway Bay offers some intriguing options. There's fishing – one of Bruce's personal passions. There are also galleries of Aboriginal rock art in the sandstone outcrops, sensational birdlife, croc-spotting trips and, to the west, Shell Beach consists of nothing but cockle and scallop shells, bleached by the sun and stacked into great drifts. Nearby is a deep, green-water swimming hole at the foot of a vast amphitheatre with red walls 80-metres high where you can hover in the cool, dark water, watched by the water monitors that give the pool its name.

At the absolute top of the list is the trip along the King George River – one of Australia's supreme scenic cruises. Aboard the lodge's 13-metre cruiser, *Diamond Lass*, it's just a short journey east into the gaping mouth of the King George River. For the next 11 kilometres, the cruiser follows a narrowing gorge, hemmed in by giant walls that rear high overhead. Finally, the vessel rounds a bend and brings you face-to-face with the awesome majesty of the King George Falls. During the wet season, all sound is drowned out, all vision blurred by the swirling mist.

Directly off the bow the white curtain of the waterfall pumps foam and fury as it dumps tonnes of water per second from the lip 80 metres overhead. Then suddenly, the sound and the fury are over. A couple of months after the end of the wet season, the King George River dries to a trickle and the falls cease. Only a dark stain on the red walls marks the trail of the waterfall down the rock face – and now, instead of the roar of exploding water, it's the silence that resonates. This is a trip you won't forget in a long time.

THE BUSH CAMP AT FARAWAY BAY

LOCATION: On the Kimberley coast, about 300 kilometres north-west of Kununurra.

GETTING THERE: Via light aircraft from Kununurra, about a 70-minute trip, followed by a 15-minute drive to the lodge.

WHAT'S INCLUDED: All meals, transfers from the airstrip, beer and wines and activities, including day trips, guided fishing, rock art tours and walks.

MAKING THE MOST OF IT: Bring sun protection, lots of film, non-slip sandals that don't mind salt water and any favourite fishing gear, but leave the tuxedo at home. Faraway Bay Bush Camp is open between Easter and mid-October.

CONTACT: Outback Encounter
33 Queen Street, Thebarton
South Australia, 5031, Australia
Telephone + 61 8 **8354 4405**
Facsimile + 61 8 **8354 4406**
Email info@outbackencounter.com
Website www.outbackencounter.com

HIDDEN VALLEY FOREST RETREAT

Deep in the forests of the Margaret River region lies luxurious accommodation that resonates with wild sensations.

Eco-friendly lodges in a perfect setting that exude character.

DAWN BRINGS A special moment to Hidden Valley Forest Retreat. Peering from the warm cocoon of your king-size bed, the rising sun sparkles on the window dew in a nimbus of golden light.

Outside, the forest is waking up. A kookaburra sounds its manic morning call, green wings flash through the trees and rustling noises sound from the undergrowth – perhaps a bandicoot, or the possum that scampered down from its tree last night to stand enquiringly outside your window.

Even by Australian standards, the south-west region of Western Australia is cast in a separate mould. Just north of the wine capital of Margaret River, enclosed by dark woodland where stray sunbeams spotlight the forest floor, Hidden Valley Forest Retreat is the perfect place to make the most of the experience.

"I'd been brought up in Papua New Guinea," says Anne Marie Lynch, the energetic mother of three who is the driving force behind Hidden Valley. "I spent my childhood in a house that gave you a wonderful sense of the rich environment all around. It was such a happy memory that I wanted to create something of the same feeling in the south-west. As soon as I set eyes on Hidden Valley, I knew it was the place. I saw it in the morning, and by the next day, I'd signed the papers on the sale."

Anne Marie Lynch is the driving force behind Hidden Valley Forest Retreat, a series of five eco-friendly lodges in a woodland setting.

She established a vineyard, producing succulent maroon table grapes, but Hidden Valley's accommodation potential was obvious, and Anne Marie decided to create self-contained accommodation for a small number of guests. Ecological integrity was a high priority. The stands of marri, red gum, banksia and jarra on the 60 hectare site are a precious asset in an area that has been carved up for agriculture, providing a habitat for thousands of birds and native animals.

The builders were not allowed to work more than one metre from the edge of each of the five retreats she created to minimise impact on the surrounding forest. No dogs were permitted on the site to disturb the native animals. The lodges themselves are raised on piles. Raised boardwalks project from each retreat into the surrounding bushland like runways, inviting you out to shady platforms with teak chairs from where you can relax and soak up the sounds and smells.

The result is sublime – five self-contained lodges that bring style and sophistication into the heart of the forest.

A vineyard on the property produces succulent maroon table grapes. The lodges have not disturbed the ecology of the area – each is set on piles and accessed by raised boardwalks.

Make yourself at home in chic retreats that ooze character and charm.

THE LODGES ARE pure urban-chic, seamlessly merging the functions of kitchen, dining room and bedroom. Each of the retreats was designed by Anne Marie and each hints at her keen sense of the environment, as well as her cool, contemporary aesthetics.

Corrugated iron, rammed earth, glass and timber are the essential architectural elements. Floors are split bamboo, a sound system glows softly from a recessed wall slot and there's a nod to Philip Stack in the bathroom, yet each lodge is cosy as well as chic.

There's a pot-bellied stove for chilly evenings, a king-size bed and a heated tiled floor in the bathroom. The bathrooms in the two Eco Lodges have all the privacy of a goldfish bowl, but so secluded is each in its cloistered, woodsy domain that only the possums will ever know. Both the Eco Lodges have interior spa baths, while the other three have interior showers and spa baths set into their decks.

The shining, stainless-steel kitchen has everything needed to whip up a feast in the wilderness. There's a Smeg microwave, Fisher and Paykel dishwasher and cooktop, plus all the accessories, crockery, cutlery and glassware you'd expect to find in a quality kitchen. On the deck outside is a barbecue. Tea and coffee are supplied, and provisions for a full-size breakfast are delivered to your door each afternoon – eggs, bacon, cereal, yoghurt, orange juice, fresh fruit and preserves. Or, if you'd rather someone else did the cooking, Anne Marie has a talented chef at her command, with a choice of menus including a fine selection of local seafood.

The lodges are cosy as well as chic and feature barbecues on their decks and generous use of glass. Their bathrooms offer bush outlooks without compromising on contemporary style.

The south-west landscape features wonderful beaches, such as Hamlin Bay, plentiful native wildlife and the ubiquitous grass tree.

A wonderful premier wine region bounded by superb beaches and forests.

IN ITS FORESTS, vineyards and extravagantly beautiful coastline, the south-west region of Western Australia is a celebration of the great outdoors.

Pre-eminent among those attractions are the Margaret River wineries. This is one of Australia's premier winegrowing regions, acclaimed for its ability to produce wines of astonishing finesse and longevity. There are 130 wineries here, and a tasting tour is essential to the full experience of the region. Hidden Valley Forest Retreat is located at the northern border of the Margaret River vineyards. From here, the vineyards unfurl across the slowly undulating landscape, marching in meticulous ranks all the way to the town of Margaret River and beyond.

However, the wineries are only a part of the area's broad repertoire. The Margaret River itself is a frisky, free-spirited stream with a raging waterfall about two kilometres upstream from the Caves Road Bridge, Turn west toward the sea at any point along Caves Road and the mellow hills give way to a wild, flayed coastline where the tea trees have been wrestled into arthritic shapes by a wind that sprints all the way from the Cape of Good Hope.

From Yallingup, a short drive north-east of Hidden Valley, Caves Road parallels the coast, swooping through luscious, rolling farmlands and canyons of karri trees that lock arms overhead in a lacy canopy. The wildflowers in this region have evolved colours and forms that are found nowhere else on Earth, epitomised by the ubiquitous grass tree, *Xanthorrhoea preissii*, which sprouts a dense clump of fibrous wands, often from a fire-blackened stump. Come spring, and the landscape erupts in an exotic show of orange banksias, vivid yellow wattle and kangaroo paws.

The Leeuwin-Naturaliste National Park, which runs for 120km along this coast, is a favourite with fishermen, walkers and surfers, who come here to experience sublime scenery as well as one of the country's legendary surf breaks. Beyond Margaret River, Caves Road bounds south, slowing briefly as it winds through luminous ramrods of white-trunked karri trees at Boranup Forest. The road ends at Hamlin Bay, where the stout piles of a disintegrating pier frame a quiet bay where darting rays cast dark shadows on the mottled sands.

A highlight of the Margaret River calendar is the Leeuwin Estate Concerts, held outdoors each February. Since they began with a performance by the London Philharmonic Orchestra in 1985, the concerts have attracted performers as disparate as Ray Charles, Julio Iglesias, kd lang, Dame Kiri Te Kanawa and Sting.

OUTBACK
ENCOUNTER
PORTFOLIO
MEMBER

PERTH
Fremantle
Mandurah
Indian Ocean
WESTERN AUSTRALIA
Bunbury
Bussell Highway
Dunsborough
South Western Highway
Margaret River
Busselton
Bridgetown
HIDDEN VALLEY
Brockman Highway
Vasse Highway

HIDDEN VALLEY FOREST RESORT

LOCATION: 250km south of Perth.

GETTING THERE: An airstrip is located 20 minutes away and charter flights can be arranged, but a vehicle is essential for exploring the area. Perth is a three-hour drive.

WHAT'S INCLUDED: Breakfast.

MAKING THE MOST OF IT: Dress is country-style casual. Take footwear for forest and rock walking and beach towel and swimming costume for those marvellous beaches. The towns of Margaret River and Busselton, about 20 minutes away in opposite directions, have plenty of dining options as well as all essential services.

CONTACT: Outback Encounter
33 Queen Street, Thebarton
South Australia, 5031, Australia
Telephone + 61 8 **8354 4405**
Facsimile + 61 8 **8354 4406**
Email info@outbackencounter.com
Website www.outbackencounter.com

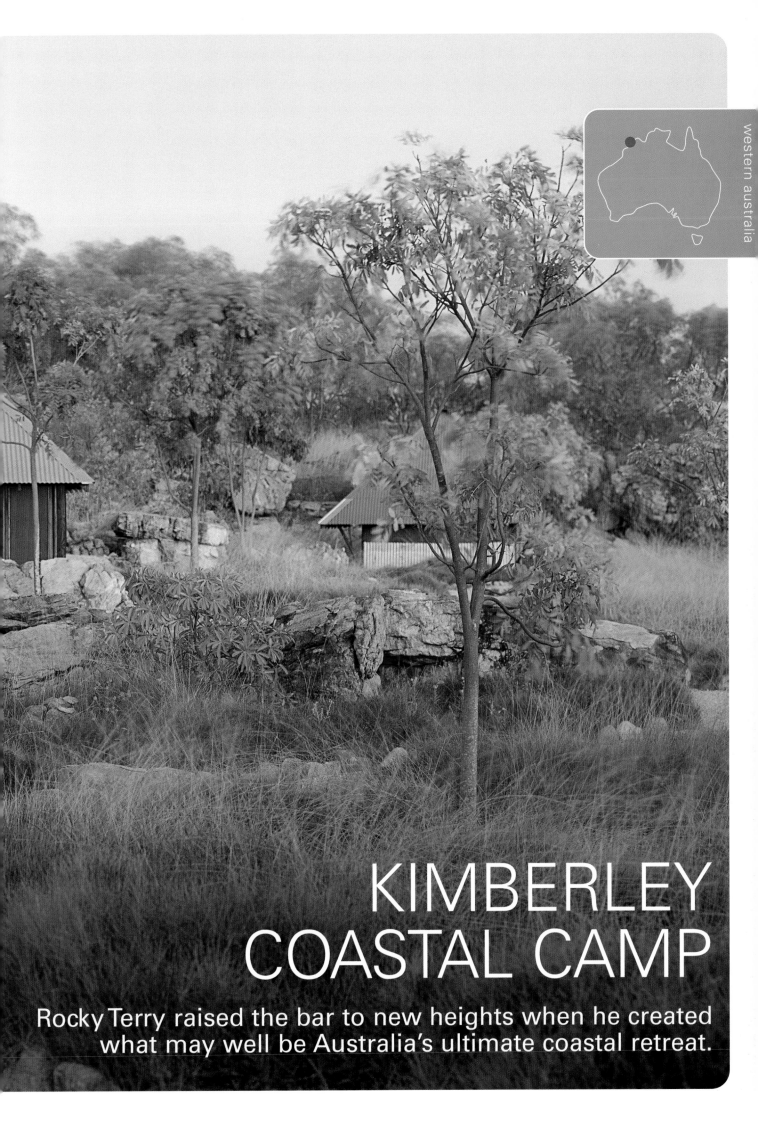

KIMBERLEY COASTAL CAMP

Rocky Terry raised the bar to new heights when he created what may well be Australia's ultimate coastal retreat.

The perfect beach house in one of the most amazing places on earth.

Rocky Terry and Bella Harding have crafted a distinctive experience that unleashes the full flavours of one of the most majestic parts of the Australian coastline.

THE JOURNEY TO Kimberley Coastal camp is a series of ever more adventurous airborne steps – jet aircraft to single-engine Cessna to helicopter – and there to meet you when you finally touch down at a beach of finely crushed seashells is a man with a pirate's beard and a shirt with the sleeves hacked off and a wheelbarrow. This is Rocky Terry, who, together with his partner, Bella Harding, just happens to own the perfect beach house. Over the next few days, they will choreograph an experience that involves fishing, food, hilarious conversation, art, music and wildlife in one of the most amazing places on earth.

It would be hard to find anywhere more at ease with its surroundings. The camp sits on a headland overlooking Port Warrender at the southern end of Admiralty Gulf, a broad, indentation in Australia's north-west coast. On one side, the camp is encircled by Mackerel Point, which throws a long, lazy arm into the sea. The colours run in arpeggio through the high notes, sharpening the sense of expectation. Set among peroxide blonde clumps of spinifex, the creamy sandstone outcrops that dominate the scenery are veined with rust; the beaches, paths and floors are seashells, bleached by the sun to a blinding white and soft and natural on the feet; the sea is a solid band of turquoise.

Set on a gentle rise close to the sea is The Shed, a big, breezy pavilion with stout posts supporting a high roof of corrugated iron, which serves as the camp's social nucleus – dining room, lounge, library, tackle room, expedition base, office, lookout, kitchen and bar. When they're not out on fishing, walking or art expeditions – 'tour' is far too tame for what happens here – guests spend much of their day here, lounging around on the couches, playing boule, absorbing the atmosphere and the smells that waft from the kitchen. Every now and again, the calm is punctuated by a sea eagle that swoops down to collect the bits of leftover fish that are laid out for it. Another shy but entertaining visitor is 'George', a wild dingo that often appears around mealtimes. Off to one side is a small swimming pool, since the sea is strictly off limits due to the abundance of species that are higher up the food chain than you are.

The decor is unique and eccentric. All around The Shed there are collections of found objects – shells, coral, driftwood, a bleached crocodile's head, a hat tree and miscellaneous bits of ironmongery – all wrought with a rich patina of salt, time and sea, and grouped together as unselfconscious sculptures that provide endless fascination. Hoisted 10 metres up to the top of a massive sandstone boulder is an ancient bathtub, although Rocky has yet to install the plumbing.

The appeal of Kimberley Coastal Camp challenges the accepted notions. If airconditioning, plush carpets, room service and spas matter, this is not the place for you. On the other hand, if you're susceptible to style, charisma, character and charm, Kimberley Coastal Camp is five-star all the way. This is a barefoot paradise, pure and simple.

Five-star doesn't just mean where you sleep – it's the whole experience that makes this place so special.

Bella Harding brings passion and flair to her cooking, with some of the freshest fish you'll ever taste, while the guest gazebos leave only the lightest of footprints on their surroundings.

THERE'S NOTHING TOO plush about the sleeping arrangements at Kimberley Coastal Camp. Scattered among the red sandstone and spinifex, there are half a dozen gazebos that consist of corrugated iron to waist level, then mosquito netting that rises to a corrugated iron roof. Inside each is a lamp, a fan and a king-size bed. Floors are crushed seashells, but as a concession to the feet, there's a rug. In this climate it's the perfect beach house – simple, stylish and completely open to the sea breezes and the sighing sound of waves on the beach. Anchored against a sandstone face, in open-topped, corrugated iron cubicles that are furnished with driftwood towel rails, the showers look like something out of an eclectic design magazine, a happy marriage between functionalism and environment.

Food is an unexpected joy. Bella is a passionate and accomplished cook who regularly works miracles in The Shed's open kitchen. During her wide-ranging travels she has absorbed influences from the Mediterranean, the Middle East and Asia, turning out wonders that range from pizzas garnished with thin slices of potato and rosemary and drizzled with olive oil to Greek-style salads with haloumi cheese to fish dishes that dance a tango with the taste buds.

Step back in time and imagine just who could have painted the mysterious Bradshaw rock art.

OUTBACK ENCOUNTER PORTFOLIO MEMBER

GIVEN THE NATURAL abundance of the inlet where the camp lies, it's to be expected that this was once a habitation site. In particular, the rock overhangs around the camp contain some exquisite examples of Bradshaw art. Dated back 30,000 years, these fluid, stylised figures are one of the great enigmas of Kimberley art, disowned by the local Aboriginal people. Unlike mainstream Aboriginal art – which mostly depicts animals and spiritual figures – the focus of Bradshaw art is elongated human figures, often in dynamic poses and wearing elaborate decorations on their arms and ankles and in their hair. The artists who painted the Bradshaws will perhaps never be known to us, but they suggest a society of leisure and sophistication – which only increases the potent spell that these works cast on the imagination. Once seen, it's hard not to become an addict.

Birdwatchers, photographers, artists and hikers will find plenty to keep them occupied, but it's extremely unlikely that you'll go to Kimberley Coastal camp and not go fishing. If you didn't know already, the huge stack of fishing tackle that greets you at the entrance to The Shed says it all. The gulf is legendary for its barramundi, which run strong in April and May, at the end of the runoff. At other times of the year there are fingermark, mangrove jack, tuna, barracuda, giant trevally, coral trout and shark, and plenty of mud crabs among the mangroves. Only the trophy fish and those required for the dinner table are kept – which means most of the day is catch-and-release, but now and again a fish will be filleted on board, dunked in a marinade of citrus juice, vinegar and coriander, left for 15 minutes and voila – poisson cru.

Although it's legendary for its fishing, the Bradshaw art around the camp is sublime, and some of the world's oldest, while the rock platforms are grooved from the scrapings where Aboriginal hunters once sharpened their spears.

KIMBERLEY COASTAL CAMP

LOCATION: On Admiralty Gulf, north-west of Kununurra.

GETTING THERE: Light aircraft from Kununurra to Mitchell Plateau airstrip (no facilities, one-hour flight), then helicopter (15 mins) to the camp.

WHAT'S INCLUDED: All meals, transfers, fishing gear, boat trips, guided walks and other activities.

MAKING THE MOST OF IT: Pack light for warm, sunny days, but don't forget sun protection and non-slip footwear. Soft drinks are provided, and alcohol can be ordered when you book. The camp is open between April and mid-October.

CONTACT: Outback Encounter
33 Queen Street, Thebarton
South Australia, 5031, Australia
Telephone + 61 8 **8354 4405**
Facsimile + 61 8 **8354 4406**
Email info@outbackencounter.com
Website www.outbackencounter.com

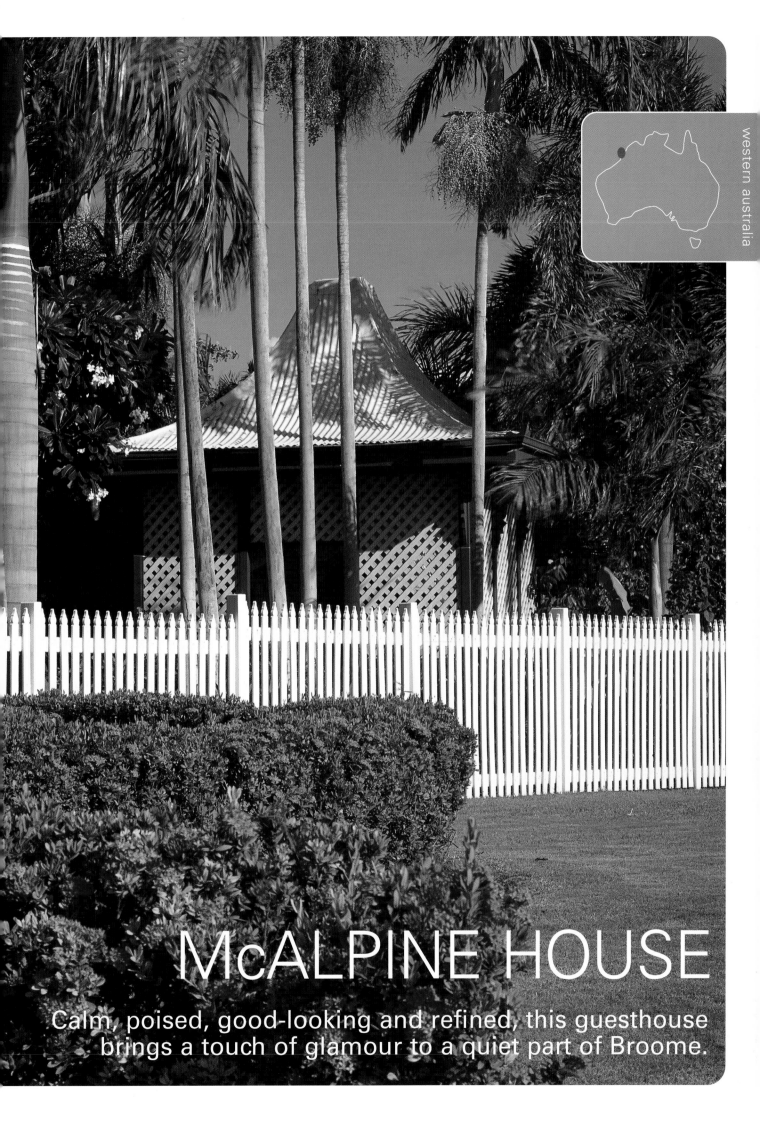

McALPINE HOUSE

Calm, poised, good-looking and refined, this guesthouse brings a touch of glamour to a quiet part of Broome.

The tea house is a great spot to idle away an afternoon – or there are the antique couches on the broad verandahs.

Soothing and relaxing in a unique tropical environment with wonderful history.

IT'S EASY TO miss McAlpine House. Buried behind a screen of palm trees in a suburban location in a quiet part of Broome, there's nothing about the façade to suggest the treasures that lie within.

Located just a 15-minute walk from the town centre – and even less to Town Beach – McAlpine House consists of a series of timber pavilions set around an opal-blue pool. The architecture borrows heavily from the motifs that have evolved uniquely over the years in this hothouse town, which owes its very existence to the pearling industry. The deep, dark verandahs are enclosed with latticework to allow the breeze through while providing privacy. Windows cut into the latticework swing open from the bottom, a style that the town has made its own. Roofs and even walls are made from corrugated iron, the only building material that resists termites and defies the intense tropical downpours. The effect is soothing and instantly relaxing.

Instantly, McAlpine House feels like a home. Hardly anyone bothers to lock their doors, and in fact many guests sleep with their doors open, preferring the silky night air and the sound of the breeze in the palm fronds to the comfort of airconditioning.

Simplicity is key here. The green and white colour scheme harmonises perfectly with the twining greenery, the arching palm trees and the sound of bird noises from the aviary in the background. Splashes of colour provide stylish accents. Like Broome itself, McAlpine House revels in a composite of multicultural influences. There are Javanese couches, rattan chairs, and beside the pool, an Indian couch suspended from chains.

McAlpine House is a mirror of Broome's own exotic history. Built in 1910, it was originally the home of one of Broome's pearling masters, the men who controlled the trade in mother-of-pearl that was for many years the town's economic mainstay. In 1982, it became the home of Lord Alistair McAlpine of West Green, who provided the inspiration, enthusiasm and much of the cash for the transformation of Broome in the 1980s.

While maintaining the original character of the house, McAlpine carried out extensive renovations and planted the tropical gardens. It was also McAlpine – a passionate ornithologist – who installed the aviary that still provides the background music to the house, as well as its icon, the eclectus parrot. In the 1990s, the house was sold again, rejuvenated and opened as an exclusive guesthouse, and today there is nowhere better to base yourself while experiencing this colourful, charismatic town and its staggeringly beautiful surroundings.

Cool and relaxed, the free-flowing design blurs the distinctions between inside and out.

THERE ARE JUST six rooms at McAlpine House, and no two are the same. Located beside the swimming pool, the Pearlers Rooms are the original part of the house, two comfortable suites with French doors that open to a private verandah.

The McAlpine Suite is large and luscious, with a four-poster bed and an old-fashioned claw-foot bath as well as a shower in the tiled bathroom. On the floor above, the two Library Rooms are quiet and cosy, with immediate access to the Library with its patrician airs, glossy furnishings and plump couches. The Tree House is a touch of pure whimsy – a guest room hoisted high into the trees, above a jungle of ferns filled with exotic birds.

Each suite is equipped with airconditioning as well as a ceiling fan, and each has its own ensuite bathroom. With the exception of the Tree House,

each of the suites opens to a broad, shady enclosed verandah. This is virtually an extension of your room, and the temptation to curl up here on the couches for an afternoon of reading or daydreaming is too much to resist.

Each morning a sumptuous breakfast is laid out in the dining pavilion to one side of the swimming pool. While Broome has no shortage of delectable cafes and restaurants, one of the best places to eat in town is right at McAlpine House, especially in the evening when the lights are twinkling around the pool.

Guests are welcome to have a take-away meal from one of the local restaurants by the pool or on your verandah or under the mango tree – and the manager will happily offer advice, or even deliver your meal. If you're in the mood for a slap-up feast, you can even have your very own chef imported for the occasion. ⬂

Meals can be enjoyed poolside, and there are plenty of spots for hanging around beneath the palm trees. The upstairs libraries are hushed get-aways, the breakfast table deserves serious attention – or you can just hole up in your elegant suite.

Broome is a town that revels in its surroundings and pearling pioneers.

TUCKED AWAY IN its secluded north-west corner of the continent, Broome is a likeable, languid cocktail of warmth, unbuttoned living and rainbow colours. The town revels in its surroundings, which border on the realms of fantasy. Cable Beach is 22 kilometres of powder-white sand that stretches to the horizon at extreme low tide, at its best in the evening, when camels convey visitors on a sunset trek. At Ganthaeume Point – where the sea dashes against a surreal collection rust-red rock stacks – a low tide exposes dinosaur footprints 120 million years old.

Broome is Australia's pearl capital. Just before World War I, the town's 400 pearling luggers and 3500 divers produced 80 percent of the world's pearl shell, which was mostly used for buttons. The industry relied on divers from tropical Asia, especially from the Philippines, Malaya and Japan, and their food, architecture and genes are woven into the fabric of modern Broome. More recently, the pearl industry has revived on the strength of the cultured pearl farms along the Kimberley coastline, and shopping for pearls at the elegant Paspaley shop in the town centre – or just pressing your nose against the window – remains one of Broome's prime attractions.

High among Broome's nightlife attractions is Sun Pictures, an open-air movie theatre that is also the world's oldest operating outdoor picture garden. Buy your ticket at the front, invest in a chocolate-coated ice cream cone and settle down in a deck chair to watch the film under the stars.

Broome is also the western gateway to the Kimberley, the wild, arid plateau that stretches for hundreds of kilometres to the east. A journey across the Kimberley will take a week at least, but even a brief journey with one of Broome's adventure tour operators will give you a taste of this astonishing wilderness.

OUTBACK
ENCOUNTER
PORTFOLIO
MEMBER

Cape Leveque

INDIAN
OCEAN

Beagle Bay

WESTERN
AUSTRALIA

Derby

McALPINE HOUSE

Broome

Great Northern Highway

McALPINE HOUSE

LOCATION: One kilometre from Broome town centre.

GETTING THERE: Broome Airport is less than a five-minute drive away, with direct flights from all major Australian cities. The nearest city with an international airport is Perth, a three-hour flight away.

WHAT'S INCLUDED: Breakfast.

MAKING THE MOST OF IT: Expect warm to very warm conditions all year round. The wet season months of November to March are especially hot and humid, and many activities are closed. The most comfortable season is between May and September.

CONTACT: Outback Encounter
33 Queen Street, Thebarton
South Australia, 5031, Australia
Telephone + 61 8 **8354 4405**
Facsimile + 61 8 **8354 4406**
Email info@outbackencounter.com
Website www.outbackencounter.com

TRUE NORTH

A sensational way to see an inspiring strip
of Australia's rugged north-west coast.

The Kimberley – a land of wild treasures where Mother Nature has been left to run riot.

EVEN BY THE lofty standards that apply in the Kimberley, Eagle Falls is a singular place. Located in the Vansittart Bay region, on Australia's remote north-west coastline, an unnamed river tumbles through rock pools that are separated by waterfalls as it steps down from the escarpment to the plain below.

This is a Garden of Eden in tropical mode – a series of black ledges iced with foaming water gushing through rock swimming holes that are edged with pandanus palms and cradled between rough, red walls. As natural swimming holes go, it doesn't get any better than this, yet only a privileged few will ever see it. Eagle Falls lies about 10 kilometres upstream from the river mouth, and the river is too shallow for even a small craft. Getting here would mean a long and arduous slog through rocky scrubland. But if you happen to have a helicopter, it's only a five-minute flight from the coast – and a helicopter is just one of the things that distinguishes a cruise aboard *True North*.

Launched at the end of 2004, this sparkling, 50-metre vessel is the latest addition to cruising along the Kimberley coastline, and from bow to stern,

The waterfalls of the Kimberley coast are some of Australia's most amazing sights – but the journey is easier if you've got a helicopter to take you there.

True North is nothing less than sensational. The vessel was purpose-built to the specifications of Craig Howson, who has been operating charter cruises through these waters since 1987, and his experience shows in every detail.

The 36-passsenger cruiser is fully airconditioned and equipped with exceptional leisure facilities for a vessel of this size. There's a large lounge/library with a bar, internet facility, plasma TVs and surround sound system and a big dining room on the deck below. There's also a forward observation lounge and access to the forward deck. *True North* carries several tenders, which allow passengers to take advantage of the broad range of activities that each area offers – whether it's fishing, exploring Aboriginal rock art sites or hiking along the river gorges. Best of all though is the helicopter.

True North is the only vessel cruising the Kimberley coast that carries its own chopper, giving easy access to rock art sites, fishing holes and swimming spots that would be virtually impossible to reach by any other means. And it must be said, a personal helicopter brings a whole new dimension to cruising in the Kimberley.

By the time you've swum in the cool, dark water at Eagle Falls, you'll find the crew has prepared a spectacular seafood barbecue, complete with iced drinks and chilled wine.

Something else that sets *True North* apart is its crew. They are young, lively, professional and passionate. Many passengers describe the cruise as a process of being absorbed into a big, happy family who just happen to live aboard the perfect vessel in one of the most amazing places on earth. Together – ship, crew and Kimberley coastline – they make an experience like no other. ↘

With two chefs and exquisite seafood on demand, every meal is a celebration.

CABINS ABOARD *True North* come in several different configurations. Explorer and River Class cabins have king-size beds that can convert to singles, while the Ocean Class twins feature roomy single beds. Whichever cabin you choose, you'll have plush quarters with your own ensuite bathroom, individual airconditioning, a TV monitor with a DVD player, satellite phone and heaps of stowage space.

Food is not usually a high point aboard small expeditionary cruise vessels, yet the two chefs who work in the galley turn out three delicious and not-so-square meals every day. Fresh from the water, seafood dominates the menu, and chances are you won't taste fresher crab, fingermark and barramundi than here. A light, Asian-inspired touch plays through the menu, complemented by the small but fine selection of wines available on board. Breakfast includes cereals, juices and bread, followed by a hot dish – which might be eggs benedict or mushroom omelettes. There's even an espresso machine in the bar, so addicts of urban-strength caffeine need never feel deprived.

The bar is a favourite spot in the evenings, a pleasant and convivial gathering place for an hour or so, when most passengers lounge around on the couches or head out onto one of the decks to watch the sun set over the water. With the cocktail of the day or a well-shaken martini in hand, it's moments like this that make the cruise aboard *True North* special. ↘

Food is one of the unexpected highlights of the voyage aboard *True North*. Suites are stylish and luxuriously appointed, while even the dining room has a blue view.

Whether it's fishing, a bush barbeque, Aboriginal rock art, shark feeding, soaking up the sights – or a thorough soaking – every day brings a whole new feast of activities.

On board or on shore, it's all action and appeal.

EVERY DAY BRINGS something different. The daily program is delivered to your suite while you're at dinner – along with the pillow chocolate. A typical day begins early. Breakfast is served at 6:30am, but there are usually a few passengers already buttering their raisin toast and raring to go by that time.

The Kimberley coastline is one of Australia's greatest natural treasures, an astonishing wilderness of wild rivers, waterfalls, red cliffs and crystalline beaches that stand stark against a teeming blue sea. In many places the rock outcrops are daubed with Aboriginal rock art, animals and mythological figures that are some of the oldest examples of artistic expression found anywhere on Earth, including the mysterious and captivating Bradshaw art – sinuous, dynamic figures that, according to some experts, hint at a separate origin from the main corpus of Aboriginal rock art.

The fishing is exceptional. The catch includes giant trevally, coral trout, mangrove jack, fingermark, mackerel and tuna, and keen anglers can expect to spend several hours a day with rod in hand if they choose, either fishing off rocks along the rivers or trolling.

The local wildlife is not especially abundant, but it's breathtaking. Often there are crocodiles lurking off the vessel in the morning, which is just one reason why it's not possible to swim from the ship.

There are brahminy kites wheeling against the sky and often a shark or two circling off the transom.

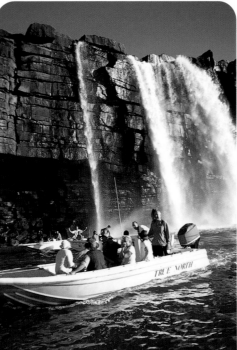

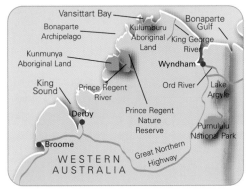

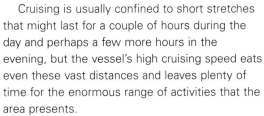

Cruising is usually confined to short stretches that might last for a couple of hours during the day and perhaps a few more hours in the evening, but the vessel's high cruising speed eats even these vast distances and leaves plenty of time for the enormous range of activities that the area presents.

One of the highlights of the cruise is the trip along the King George River. From the time the vessel crosses the sandbar at the river mouth, this is a fantastic journey between sheer red rock walls that become progressively narrower until the vessel finally reaches the King George Falls. Here, the captain edges the vessel closer and closer until the bow is right under the falls. The temptation is all too much, and within a couple of minutes, half the passengers and crew are standing under the pounding water, laughing hilariously as they are drenched beneath the torrent that thunders down from high overhead, which is probably the most memorable outdoor shower you'll ever have.

TRUE NORTH

LOCATION: *True North* makes regular cruises along the Kimberley coast from Broome to Wyndham between March and September.

GETTING THERE: Cruises begin in Broome, which has frequent air services from all major Australian cities, or in Wyndham, about a one-hour drive from Kununurra, which has daily flights from Broome and Darwin.

WHAT'S INCLUDED: All meals and activities, but helicopter flights incur a surcharge.

MAKING THE MOST OF IT: The most comfortable period for cruising is May to September, with the earlier months recommended when the waterfalls are still flowing. Take lots of t-shirts.

CONTACT: Outback Encounter
33 Queen Street, Thebarton
South Australia, 5031, Australia
Telephone + 61 8 **8354 4405**
Facsimile + 61 8 **8354 4406**
Email info@outbackencounter.com
Website www.outbackencounter.com

BULLO RIVER STATION

The story comes true on a rugged cattle station
made famous by author Sara Henderson.

The flight from Darwin to Bullo River Station confirms the extraordinary nature of Australia's tropical north.

STRETCHING BELOW YOUR wings is a landscape that has been cast in the furnace – seared brown rocks, open savannah and an eternity of emptiness. It is a landscape that seems to have swollen to outlandish proportions. The Victoria River is a huge brown python that slithers toward the sea over mud flats and mangrove swamps, its tributaries and smaller channels joining like the roots of a giant tree. Among these branches is the Bullo River, which gives its name to one of the classic experiences of Top End travel, Bullo River Station. Your aircraft comes in to land in a cloud of dust, whizzes past a couple of surprised wallabies and several stockhorses that stand and watch, then a flock of corellas takes to the air like a cloud of white snowflakes and settles again, and finally your aircraft taxis through the gate and pulls up at the front of the homestead. Welcome to Bullo River Station.

This is the very essence of a Top End cattle station, half a million acres of grassy plains with 8000 Brahman-cross cattle and many more wallabies, brown rivers where crocodiles lurk on the muddy banks, rugged hills inscribed with Aboriginal artwork, gushing steams and crystal-clear swimming holes, termite mounds, boab trees, stockhorses and wild buffalo.

Bullo River Station is also a literary experience. The property provided the inspiration for one of Australia's best-selling authors, Sara Henderson, whose story of the trials and tribulations of establishing and operating a cattle station in the wild frontier with her American husband, Charles, captured the hearts and imaginations of the nation. These days, the property has passed to her eldest daughter, Marlee Ranacher, and her husband, Franz, and it is their energy and passion that adds a fascinating dimension to any visit.

For the visitor, this is not a choreographed experience, but one that changes according to the dictates of station life – which revolves around cattle. There is no such thing as a typical day at Bullo River Station, but during the course of your stay, you can expect to go fishing and catch something for your photo album, see a crocodile or two at surprisingly close quarters, visit an Aboriginal rock art site that depicts a rainbow serpent from the Dreamtime, learn to swing a billy and to crack a bullwhip, swap a few stories around the dinner table, go fishing again and probably laugh quite a lot. Bullo is an extraordinary place, and having Marlee and Franz and their team of co-workers to show you around will be among the fondest memories you take back home.

The lazy snake of the Bullo River weaves toward the sea, carving through plains where wild buffalo roam, giant lizards stalk and where thirsty cattlework is unceasing.

Local ingredients don't come fresher than wild Barra hauled straight from the river.

GATHER ROUND, JOIN in the fun and meet some great outback characters.

Guest accommodation is located in a large, purpose-built annexe within the ring of green lawns that surrounds the homestead. There are 12 modern, comfortable, airconditioned rooms in total, each with its own ensuite. Rooms are serviced daily, and they provide a cool and comfortable refuge for the times when you're not out riding the wild ranges or fishing for barramundi.

Food has always played an important part in station life, and Bullo River Station honours the tradition while bringing a modern touch to the table, with robust meals that appear three times a day. Fresh meat and freshly-caught fish are staples, as well as salads and home-made bread and cakes, all prepared by the station cook who is one of the most valued members of the Bullo team.

Barbeques are a regular occurrence, and here, where the beef is hormone-free and raised only on wild pasture grasses, this is some of the finest, freshest beef you'll ever taste. Breakfast and dinner are usually served outside, at the big table at the front of the homestead, while lunch is often a picnic, eaten at a rock-lined swimming hole or out at a stockcamp where the ringers are busy with the cattle.

The welcome at the sprawling homestead is expansive, in the best traditions of the Top End, while Franz Ranacher hoists something for the dinner table.

From mustering cattle to plunging into the local swimming pool to gazing at Aboriginal rock art, Bullo River is not your average getaway. With co-owner Marlee Ranacher, you can expect to experience a few things you've probably never done before.

Fish to your heart's content or take a chopper to an isolated oasis.

TO STAY AT Bullo River Station is to be caught up in the energetic life of a working cattle station. Except when safety dictates otherwise, guests are usually welcome to take a front-seat view on the huge range of activities that are associated with the running of an outback cattle station, which might be anything from mustering work to branding and dehorning of cattle in the yard.

It's times like this that Marlee Ranacher's passion for her home shines through, and when she is present, the conversation revolves inevitably around the business of managing the property – a fascinating insight into a very different way of life.

There's also Evan, the former champion rodeo rider who can still roll a cigarette with one hand while clasping the reins in the other – a fascinating character with a rich fund of stories and a source of great delight, especially if there are children around. If you've ever wanted to learn how to crack a bullwhip, Evan is the ideal teacher.

The fishing is excellent, and Franz is always ready to drop a line in the river for barramundi. As well as excellent fishing, the Bullo River also has a large freshwater swimming hole. The property also has an Aboriginal art site at what was once probably an important ceremonial meeting place, bushwalks, various hunting options and bird and wildlife watching. Stargazing is a natural in the clear, dark, pollution-free skies over the property.

One of the best ways to spend an afternoon at Bullo River is a visit to Cascades. A 15-minute helicopter flight from the homestead, a spring-fed stream trickles through a sandstone cliff, carving a series of magnificent jade-green rock pools connected by waterfalls. Spending a couple of hours here, alternating between the cool water and the warm rocks, is an experience to treasure.

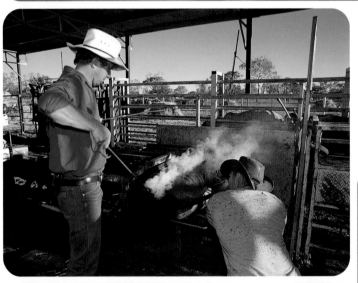

TIMOR SEA

NORTHERN TERRITORY

Katherine

Victoria River

Legune ■

BULLO RIVER STN

Bullo River ■   Timber Creek

Auvergne ■

Gregory National Park

Victoria Highway

BULLO RIVER STATION

LOCATION: In the north-west of the Northern Territory, near the Western Australian border. The nearest town is Kununurra, 200 kilometres away.

GETTING THERE: A 90-minute flight from Darwin or 30 minutes from Kununurra. Victoria Highway passes Bullo's front gate, then there's 75km of dirt to the homestead (often impassable in the wet season).

WHAT'S INCLUDED: All meals, including beer and wine, all activities at the property. Helicopter charters are available for an additional charge.

MAKING THE MOST OF IT: Take loose but durable clothing and sturdy footwear. Bullo River Station is open between February and late November.

CONTACT: Outback Encounter
33 Queen Street, Thebarton
South Australia, 5031, Australia
Telephone + 61 8 **8354 4405**
Facsimile + 61 8 **8354 4406**
Email info@outbackencounter.com
Website www.outbackencounter.com

LONGITUDE 131°

A room with a view: stellar accommodation, with front seat views of Australia's national icon.

Strong colours and striking compositions on every side – whether it's the natural surroundings or Longitude's luxurious tents.

Longitude 131° puts a shine on Uluru and the other splendours of the Central Australian desert.

ULURU, AS AYERS Rock is known to Australia's Aboriginal people, is Australia's most potent icon. And Australians have embraced this titanic, 350-metre high hump of scorched red sandstone as a fitting metaphor for the grandeur, the isolation, the weird other-worldliness of their island home.

Set among scorched red sand dunes covered with tufts of spinifex and desert oaks, Longitude 131° is the perfect base for exploring the majesty and the meaning of Uluru and its surroundings. This is one of the most impressive small resorts in the country, a sculpted sanctuary that strikes a dramatic pose amid the sun-blistered grandeur of its surroundings.

But for all its sophistication, the greatest asset of Longitude 131° is its proximity to Uluru. Although there are several other places to stay at Ayers Rock Resort, there is nowhere else that offers anything like the feeling of intimacy, nor the same staggering views.

Close up, the physicality of Uluru is overwhelming. No longer is it a smooth dome, but a scarred colossus with the evidence of eons of sun and rain etched on its pitted hide. Uluru has a different mood for every time of day. Pink in the early morning, it becomes rust in the blazing light of midday. At sunset, the iron-rich rock glows molten red with a slow-burning fire that seems to come from within. When it rains – a rare occurrence in this part of the world – the water cascading from the rock can colour it purple or green.

Along with its physical presence, Uluru has a spiritual dimension that cannot be ignored. Stand with your back against it, close your eyes and you can sense that there is something elemental about this hunk of rock, a connection with the very roots of life. This is a rock with power.

The local Aboriginal people, who refer to themselves as Anangu, have lived in the shadow of Uluru for perhaps 30,000 years. Nomadic hunter-gatherers who meshed their lives with the land around them, they are connected to the earth in a profound way that enables them to know where to find water in a parched landscape, where to dig for honey ants, how long ago a red kangaroo left its prints in the soft sand, and when to expect rain from a cloudless sky.

For the Anangu, Uluru resonates with sacred meaning. According to their view of the world, Uluru – and every other feature and being in the landscape – was created by giant ancestral beings who roamed the land in a period known as the Dreamtime, sculpting the rocks, the rivers and the hills. Many of the caves, hollows and scars of Uluru bear witness to those ancestors. Streaks in the rock might be blood that seeped from a wound, a line of rocks might be footprints, a particular cave might be the sleeping place of a giant lizard. There are men's areas, where women would never go or even glance, and women's sites. Only those who have been initiated to the required level will ever see the sites that are most sacred.

If you want to experience this facet of the Australian experience with style, luxury and the respect that it deserves, there is nowhere else like Longitude 131°.

Camping was
never quite like
this, but this is
something else.

THEY MIGHT CALL them "tents", but apart from the sweeping fabric roof, there is nothing in the least tent-like about the accommodation. Arrayed in two separate lines on parallel sand dunes, each tent is elevated on stilts and painted in a dramatic ochre colour. In the rooms the mood is totally, top-to-toe luscious. There's a king-size bed with crisp linen, a Bose music system, individual climate control and plump couches strategically placed for admiring the view. Shutters glide down to cover the floor-to-ceiling windows, so you can open your eyes in the morning, flick a switch and watch Uluru, glowing in the morning sun.

No other rooms at Ayers Rock Resort offer such a spectacle. Although the colour scheme is the same soothing mix of vanilla and chocolate tones, each room takes its theme from a different aspect of outback life – which might be an explorer, or an institution, such as the Royal Flying Doctor Service. Behind the bed, separated by a partition that cleverly disguises the wardrobe and mini-bar, is a gorgeous bathroom.

Food is one of the best things about Longitude 131°, and all meals and drinks are included in the tariff. The modern Australian cuisine is polished, innovative and served with style. Weather permitting, every second night Longitude 131° offers an extra special experience – Table 131 – dining under the stars.

After toasting the sunset over Uluru with a flute of champagne from an elevated position just behind the Dune House, diners are taken to a small clearing set up with tables and chairs and an outdoor kitchen where the chef prepares a delicious three-course dinner. Unless there's a bight moon to light the surroundings, it feels like a tiny island suspended in a sea of darkness, beneath a dazzling canopy of stars.

Whether it's the food, the atmosphere or your room, Longitude brings five-star brilliance to every department.

Discover the secrets of the Central Australian landscape – or just sit back and admire the view.

ULURU AND ITS surroundings have become a showcase for the desert version of the Australian outback experience, and Longitude 131° has an extensive program of guided walks and interpretative and cultural tours.

Included in the program is the Kuniya and Liru Walk, which skirts part of the base of Uluru to visit sites sacred to the Anangu people, a hike through the dramatic Walpa Gorge at Kata Tjuta, a Desert Awakenings tour to watch the sunrise over Uluru accompanied by the morning chorus of birds, and various sunset tours.

Most activities take place in the early morning and late afternoon, which makes the best use of the light for photography and filming.

The extreme ends of the day are also the most comfortable for touring and walking, which leaves the middle of the day free for relaxation, quiet

contemplation and a long lunch. All tours are in the company of expert guides who have an incredible knowledge of this landscape and its people, from the growth patterns of the spiky spinifex plants to an Aboriginal view of the constellations in the night sky. Without their knowledge, it would be almost impossible to enter this deeper and more meaningful dimension of Uluru.

Longitude 131° has a heated pool – a great spot to lounge in the middle of the day, with plenty of shade to blunt the fierce heat of the sun.

Combining the functions of dining room, library, lounge and café, the Dune House, the resort's centrepiece, is a big, elevated pavilion with the same swooping, tent-like roof as the rest of the resort. At night, the translucent roof is lit from within – a dramatic sight against the ink sky.

NORTHERN
TERRITORY

Alice Springs

Hermannsburg

Erldunda

Katatjuta
LONGITUDE 131

Uluru

LONGDITUTE 131°

LOCATION: 340 kilometres south-west of Alice Springs, and 2170 kilometres north-west of Sydney.

GETTING THERE: There are regular flights from all major Australian capital cities to Ayers Rock Airport. Complimentary coach transfers from the airport to the resort meet every scheduled flight.

WHAT'S INCLUDED: All meals, drinks and activities.

MAKING THE MOST OF IT: Dress cool and casual, but be prepared for chilly nights. Visitors in the hot summer months between November and March should restrict their sightseeing to early morning and late afternoon.

CONTACT: Outback Encounter
33 Queen Street, Thebarton
South Australia, 5031, Australia
Telephone + 61 8 **8354 4405**
Facsimile + 61 8 **8354 4406**
Email info@outbackencounter.com
Website www.outbackencounter.com

LORD'S KAKADU & ARNHEMLAND SAFARIS

For the ultimate outback experience, there's nothing better than being on safari in the pristine wonderland of the Top End.

Sab offers privileged access to some of the region's best-kept secrets.

Sab and his team really know their way around Kakadu and Arnhem Land, and have access to art sites, waterholes and wildlife that are off-limits to all but a fortunate few.

IT'S DAWN AT Sandy Billabong in Kakadu National Park and the birds are singing you from sleep, dragging you awake from the cocoon of your sleeping bag. They begin about half an hour before sunrise while the sky is still ink and the stars are fading to a memory. There's a butcherbird, the diva of the bush, working in arpeggio, and cockatoos, raucous and sharp-edged, and soft twitterings from birds that call pensively and wait for a response. And then a dingo joins in, a crooning sound that makes you wonder at first what kind of a throat is making that sound, but instinctively you know.

Unzip your tent and the rising sun is bleeding across the billabong, making silhouettes of the paperbarks and pandanus palms around its edges. A darter stands with its wings outstretched, drying them in the sun before it can plunge into the water in search of fish. This is a special moment. Although this is peak season – and although Kakadu gets several hundred thousand visitors a year – there's nobody else around you in this idyllic campsite, which is just one of the many reason for travelling with Sab Lord.

Sab has been operating tours in Kakadu and Arnhem Land for many years, and if you want to make the most of this extraordinary region, one of Sab's tours is the way to go. The main reason is the expertise that he brings to the task – the kind of expertise that will make the region come alive for you. While it's simple to pick up a hire car or campervan in Darwin and explore Kakadu on your own, you'll miss quite a lot.

The Top End is an open-air bush food larder, but it takes an expert to tell the difference between a ripe bush passionfruit and one that will give you a stomach ache. Only a knowledgeable guide can unravel the mysteries of the Aboriginal rock art, and it's fairly easy to drive past a pile of boulders without ever knowing that to the local Bininj people, these are the eggs of the Rainbow Serpent.

When it comes to showing you around the vast expanse of territory that he calls his backyard, Sab has a few persuasive advantages over other tour operators. Sab was raised on a buffalo property that has now become part of Kakadu National Park. Not only did that early experience give him a profound knowledge of the region's unique flora and fauna, it also brought him into close contact with the Aboriginal people of Kakadu. Today, Sab enjoys an intimacy with local Aboriginals that few others can match. This means he enjoys privileged access to some of the region's best-kept secrets. For example, only two operators are licensed to take tours into Arnhem Land, the huge chunk of the Northern Territory that was granted to the Aboriginal people in the 1930s. That means access to art sites, waterholes and wildlife treasures that are strictly off-limits to all but a fortunate few. And it's an Aboriginal guide Sab employs who will take you around the sites, explain their meaning and answer your questions – which raises the experience to a far more satisfying and revealing level.

Lord's Kakadu &
Arnhemland Safaris

Sab operates his tours from the comfort of a four-wheel-drive, which gives his small groups access to some of the natural highlights of the Top End.

A night or two under the stars will bring you to your senses, if they aren't already twitching with anticipation.

SAB LORD'S TOURS are ideally suited to small-group, personalised groups of two or more. All tours are flexible, and can be constructed to fit with clients' requirements. While most of his tours take place in Arnhem Land, Kakadu and Litchfield National Parks, Sab also ventures far and wide across the Top End, including the Kimberley region as far as Broome.

Clients who have experienced Arnhem Land with Sab will often come back for a more extensive look at Australia's Top End. Accommodation can either be camping or hotels and motels along the way. The hotel/motel option obviously scores higher for comfort, and a hot shower and a bed at the end of a long and dusty day can be sheer bliss, but if you want an intimate experience of the places you're seeing you should plan to spend at least a couple of nights under canvas, cooking over a campfire and wakening to the sounds of birdsong.

The vehicle Sab uses for his adventures is a comfortable, powerful Toyota four-wheel-drive which combines rugged off-road abilities with the effortless performance of a long-legged cruiser that can gallop across Australia's vast distances in record time. The Toyota seats four adults in comfort. The terrain makes it almost impossible to access some of the areas that Sab visits in larger vehicles, and for bigger groups, Sab has several other vehicles that offer the identical level of performance and comfort.

OUTBACK
ENCOUNTER
PORTFOLIO
MEMBER

What's that over there … a crocodile, yes; and have you ever seen so much birdlife, anywhere?

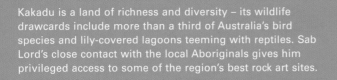

Kakadu is a land of richness and diversity – its wildlife drawcards include more than a third of Australia's bird species and lily-covered lagoons teeming with reptiles. Sab Lord's close contact with the local Aboriginals gives him privileged access to some of the region's best rock art sites.

LOCATED SOME 150 kilometres east of Darwin, Kakadu is the largest national park in Australia and the country's first to be included on the World Heritage List. This is a biological treasury, so rich and diverse that it still contains species that are yet unknown to science. For most visitors, the main attraction of the Kakadu/Arnhem Land region is wildlife. Kakadu alone is home to more than 75 species of reptiles and more than a third of all Australian bird species, with the bias toward the large and exotic. The region's enormous bird population ranges in size from the red-legged jabiru, Australia's only stork, to tiny bee-eaters and honey-eaters. Herons, cormorants, ibis and egrets stalk the wetlands, noisy flocks of scarlet-collared lorikeets and white cockatoos shriek from the treetops and whistling kites drift overhead.

As the dry season progresses, Kakadu's birds and reptiles are crammed into ever shrinking wetlands. Most spectacular of these is Yellow Waters Lagoon, a branch of the South Alligator River which becomes an open-air zoo as the waters recede during the dry season, packed with frogs, birds, snakes and the park's biggest wildlife drawcard – crocodiles. Flat-bottomed boats make regular cruises on the lagoon and it is practically guaranteed that during the two-hour cruise, you will come eyeball-to-eyeball with white egrets, brolgas, jabirus, sea eagles, jacanas, pelicans, snake birds, goannas and crocodiles.

This natural abundance provided the Aboriginal inhabitants of Kakadu with a rich source of food – while the sandstone caves and rock shelters of the Arnhem Land escarpment provided shelter. Where they camped, they daubed the walls with charcoal, clay and ochre, creating a gallery of some of mankind's oldest art and the longest continuous tradition of creative expression on the planet. More than 5000 rock-art sites have been identified in Kakadu, some of them more than 30,000 years old. The paintings at Ubirr, probably the most spectacular site, show the gradual evolution of Aboriginal rock art, from simple stick figures to complex x-ray paintings and mythological figures that indicate a rich culture of legends and dreams.

At least two days are required to explore Kakadu. Cross the East Alligator River and you enter Arnhem Land – where the experiences that await will make even Kakadu seem tame.

LORD'S KAKADU & ARNHEMLAND SAFARIS

LOCATION: Most tours begin and end in Darwin, but other options are available in the Top End.

GETTING THERE: Qantas and Virgin Blue regularly fly into Darwin.

WHAT'S INCLUDED: Pickup from accommodation or airport, all admission fees, lunch and snacks.

MAKING THE MOST OF IT: Take sturdy footwear for scrambling over rocks, sun protection and insect repellent to keep the sandflies at bay.

CONTACT: Outback Encounter
33 Queen Street, Thebarton
South Australia, 5031, Australia
Telephone + 61 8 **8354 4405**
Facsimile + 61 8 **8354 4406**
Email info@outbackencounter.com
Website www.outbackencounter.com

SEVEN SPIRIT BAY
WILDERNESS LODGE

In a magic setting at the very top of Australia sits a resort that has it all – a slice of heaven at the end of the Earth.

A remote, but polished, gem guarantees treasured memories.

All the style and cushioning of a fully-fledged resort, yet at cocktail hour the local wildlife comes calling.

SHORTLY AFTER ARRIVING at Seven Spirit Bay, you will find yourself sitting down to lunch at a table with a white tablecloth that flaps in the breeze, shaded by a canopy of palm trees and dining on food that might have come straight from a glamorous urban bistro. It might seem like a resort anywhere on the planet, but this is deceptive. Stroll along the path that winds past the swimming pool and you'll find yourself overlooking a blue bay browed with thick forest that reaches almost to the water's edge. Stay here long enough and you might well spot a large saltwater crocodile floating on the water, the dark, curvaceous backs of a pod of dolphins or the dorsal fin of a shark carving an arrow across the surface.

Seven Spirit Bay gives new meaning to the word 'remote'. The lodge is located close to the northern tip of the Cobourg Peninsula, whose stubby fingers reach into the Arafura Sea from the top of the Northern Territory. There are no roads. The only access is by air or sea. Surrounding the lodge is Garig Gunak Barlu National Park, Australia's first flora and fauna protection reserve – an acknowledgement that this is a very special place.

Despite its remoteness, Seven Spirit Bay is far more polished than anyone has a right to expect. Set amid tangled coastal forest, the lodge sits on a red cliff overlooking a curving beach above a blue water bay. At its centre is a sprawling timber building with deep verandahs and twirling ceiling fans that houses restaurant, library and lounge areas. Guest rooms – known as habitats – extend into the forest on either side.

While the lawns, tropical gardens and sense of well-ordered calm might suggest a well-heeled resort, this is more adventure lodge than soft-serve sybarite's zone. For one thing, it's limited to a maximum of about 50 guests at a time, and Seven Spirit Bay constantly reminds you that all around is wilderness. There's also a fine sense of camaraderie you won't find at most resorts. Shared experiences such as spotting a sea eagle plunging onto a fish, hooking a big barramundi – or losing one – become part of the treasured memories of each passing day, and it seems only natural that people who share a boat together also share a table at dinnertime. This process is fostered by the staff members, who are universally young, friendly, enthusiastic and thoroughly professional.

Seven Spirit Bay suits a multitude of tastes. Anglers will find snapshots for the photo album in the fish that they haul in over the side. For photographers it offers dazzling sunsets, crocodiles and birds galore and the chance to capture a few really spectacular events, such as the shark-feeding session that takes place from time to time down at the jetty. For connoisseurs of wild and remote places that have been only lightly touched by humankind, this is as wild and remote as it gets. Yet Seven Spirit Bay also comes with a soft edge, and food, comfort and style are almost as important as what nature has provided. Whatever takes you there, you'll discover a small slice of heaven – at the very ends of the Earth.

Casual elegance –
and whatever
food takes
your fancy.

The chef serves up a feast
on the shady verandah,
while guest rooms provide
cool, quiet and serenity.

SET AMONG NATURAL bushland overlooking the sea, the hexagonal-shaped habitats, as the guest accommodation is known, are just about everything you could wish for in these pristine surroundings. The habitats are spaced well apart from their neighbours, and inside there's plenty of room for the two queen-size beds in each of these cool and refreshing retreats. White shutters from floor to ceiling provide ventilation as well as privacy, and floors are polished timber for barefoot comfort. The habitats don't have ensuite bathrooms, but each has its own large, private, white-tiled bathroom, arranged in clusters of three and located just a few metres from your front door.

Mealtimes at the lodge are among the fondest memories that most guests take home – along with the wildlife and the scenery. Breakfast is a buffet-style meal with fresh fruits, yoghurt and a choice of eggs and bacon cooked to order. At lunch and dinner there's a choice of two entrées and two main courses, while dessert might be a light fruit sorbet made on the premises. There's also a good selection of beers, wines and spirits. Seafood features prominently on the menu, and

successful anglers will have their catch served at the dinner table – which might be anything from a delicious salad of mud crab to an entrée of thin slices of salmon served raw with a light, Asian-style sauce or even the celebrated barramundi. All meals are served on the shady verandah or on the terrace, overlooking the pool and the blue waters of the bay.

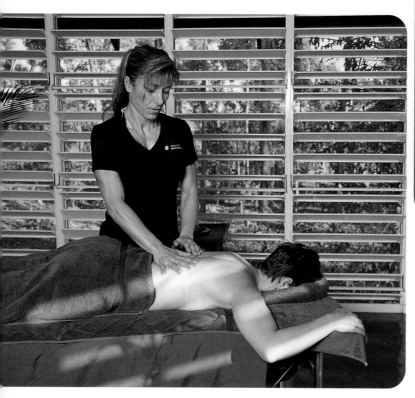

You don't have to do anything,
but you'd be mad not to.

Even novice anglers can count
on a rod-bender, while the in-
house masseuse applies the
essential soothing touch after a
day spent exploring.

WHILE THE POOL, the palm trees and the bluewater views are all perfectly good reasons to stay close to the lodge, Seven Spirit Bay is tailor-made for intrepid spirits keen to explore one of the wildest parts of northern Australia. Although it might be modest in size – just 23 guest habitats in total – the lodge is a springboard to many intriguing possibilities. Excursions along Trepang Creek, a winding waterway lined with mangroves, offer spectacular opportunities for birdwatching. Crocodile sightings are routine along Trepang Creek, and even novice anglers can count on a magnificent catch.

Fishing is a natural in these surroundings, and on any trip by water the guides will take along rods so guests can try their luck. Barramundi, mangrove jack, jewfish, giant trevally, shark and barracuda are plentiful in these abundant waters. A catch and release policy applies, but at the guide's discretion, a prime catch will sometimes appear at the dinner table. Boat trips along the coast to visit the ruins at Victoria Settlement, the ill-fated settlement established by the British in the 18th century, are another option. Within easy walking distance of the lodge, a hide set among paperbarks on the edge of a freshwater lagoon offers exceptional viewing for the many species of birds that inhabit the region. Beach walks along the crescent of fine golden sand at the front of the lodge are popular, but guests need to keep an eye out for lurking crocodiles. Sunset cocktails at a beach location are another favourite, and along the way, the guide will detour along the airfield, where there are usually a few buffalo and even wild Banteng cattle whose ancestors were imported from Indonesia in the 1800s.

The light aircraft based at the lodge gives guests a wide range of options, including one-day trips to Kakadu National Park, to the safari camp at Mount Borradaile, which is renown for its Aboriginal artwork, and to some of the remote Aboriginal settlements in Arnhem Land, where guests can purchase artworks direct from the artists themselves. And just in case this all sounds too much, there's even a masseuse on the premises, with a range of pampering treatments that will leave you relaxed, revitalised and refreshed.

Cobourg Peninsula
Gurig National Park
SEVEN SPIRIT BAY
WILDERNESS LODGE
DARWIN
Jabiru
Litchfield
National Park
Kakadu
National Park
Pine Creek
NORTHERN
TERRITORY
Katherine

SEVEN SPIRIT BAY WILDERNESS LODGE

LOCATION: 185 kilometres north-east of Darwin.

GETTING THERE: Via light aircraft from Darwin, about a 50-minute trip, followed by a 20-minute drive to the lodge. Passengers on the aircraft are restricted to 10kg of baggage. Excess baggage can be stored at the air charter operator's office.

WHAT'S INCLUDED: All meals and a selection of nature walks and activities.

MAKING THE MOST OF IT: Take casual clothing and sandals suitable for beach walking. Sensitive camera gear may need protection from fine dust and saltwater spray on excursions. Sun protection is a must. The lodge is open from mid-March to mid-December.

CONTACT: Outback Encounter
33 Queen Street, Thebarton
South Australia, 5031, Australia
Telephone + 61 8 **8354 4405**
Facsimile + 61 8 **8354 4406**
Email info@outbackencounter.com
Website www.outbackencounter.com

CAPE YORK
HELICOPTER SAFARIS

From the air, the top of Australia is a fascinating tapestry of richness. Look carefully, choose your stop and be amazed.

Cape York is a wilderness incarnate, and taking to the air is the best way to soak it all up.

LOOKING FOR A JOURNEY that will sweep you off your feet? An adventure that will lift you high and set your head spinning? Want to go to a pristine paradise where few have ever gone before, and where few will ever, ever go? Stretching north from Cairns, Cape York is the tip of the Australian mainland, a broad, stubby peninsula that tapers to a point at its northern end. It's also a wilderness incarnate, where few roads penetrate, almost uninhabited apart from a few isolated Aboriginal communities and some scattered cattle stations – and it's totally, totally amazing.

While there are several tour operators that offer trips through this remote region, one flies high above all others. As the name suggests, Cape York Helicopter Safaris takes to the air to show visitors the very best that the Cape has to offer – the finest swimming holes, the loveliest waterfalls, dunes of blinding sand that stretch to the horizon in a rippling sea and empty cays that rise like a white comma from the blue page of the sea.

The wildlife is sensational. During the flight along the coast, you'll pass over wetlands where brolgas – the tall, elegant wading bird of northern Australia – erupt from the wetlands and scatter with slow beats of their giant wings. You'll fly low over shallow waters filled with sharks and stingrays, and dusty plains studded with towering termite mounds. And crocodiles.

Basking on the muddy banks, lurking in the shallows of the rivers and charging into the water in a flurry of spray and green scales when you turn around for a closer look. These are some of the biggest crocs you'll ever see in the wild, five-metre giants some of them, the unchallenged overlords of these northern estuaries.

You'll also meet some of the amazing characters who live there. There's Walter's fishing camp, where you might be invited to sample some of Walter's mud crab, or possibly even his home-brewed whisky. There are also the Spencers, Roger and Eva, a pair of very determined escapists who live on a river near Shelburne Bay. They first came in 1985 and have lived here ever since in a modestly comfortable pole-framed house built of stout timbers with insect-proof netting all around. They tell some hilarious stories of their Robinson Crusoe life, including the time that Roger drove in to pick up some supplies with a highly poisonous brown snake curled around the brake pedal, charging down hills because he was too terrified to use the brake. Roger is also an adroit carver, the birds that he crafts from forest timbers looking as if they might burst into full-throated song at any moment. Roger will tell you that he will never leave his home in the forest. Take a ride with Cape York Helicopter Safaris and you'll know exactly what he means.

Cape York, one of Australia's least-visited corners, where the sheer scale and variety of the landscape challenges the imagination.

A choice of choppers and an
itinerary that's as open as the sky.

KNOWING THE CAPE backwards, and from all directions, is a big plus when there are so many options.

All tours with Cape York Helicopter Safaris are tailored to suit individual requirements, whether it's a two-day trip along Cape York or a complete Top End safari from Cairns to Broome. Owners Dennis and Yvonne Wallace's experience working in this region dates back to the 1960s, when they were instrumental in establishing the game fishing industry in Cairns. They know the Cape York region better than anyone, and their experience will ensure that your trip is one you won't forget in a long time. The itinerary is yours and yours alone. You decide when and where to go, how long to spend in each place and where to spend the night. Accommodation can be whatever your heart desires and purse strings allow – and there's a

great range of options available, from luxury retreats to cattle stations to coastal hideaways.

Standard workhorse for safari trips is the four-seater Robinson R44 helicopter powered by the well-tested and hugely reliable Lycoming 540 CI reciprocating engine. The fleet includes the new Raven II, which has more power, greater altitude performance, more payload, increased speed and reduced noise level. The company also has a Bell helicopter at its disposal, which carries more passengers and a greater payload. All passengers have headsets, which substantially reduces noise as well as providing instant communication with the pilot. Dennis's pilots are highly skilled and well-versed in operating helicopters in remote areas. Many obtained their experience working as muster pilots on cattle stations, which is one of the toughest proving grounds there is.

Rivers, lakes, sand dunes – and a few good reasons why you can't go swimming. The only way to see this remarkable landscape is from the air.

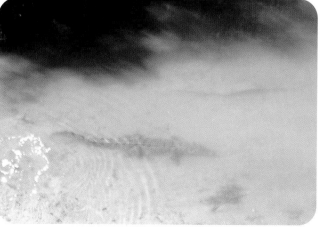

This is a land full of fascination, and the remarkable people who call it home are always ready to share some of its secrets.

As you head north up Cape York, the journey enters another dimension.

FLY WITH BIRDS of all types and colours, then keep going to wherever you wish.

Whatever your passion – wildlife, exploration, photography, beaches, botany, bizarre and exotic sights or just sightseeing – Cape York has plenty to keep you enthralled. Once past Cooktown, about an hour's flight north of Cairns, the journey enters another dimension. All roads end, all permanent habitation ceases. As far as the tip of Cape York, there are no more settlements along this coast – a distance of around 1000 kilometres.

One of the highlights is Lotus Bird Lodge, which sits on the edge of a wetland where thousands of waterbirds including magpie geese, egrets, brolgas come to feed among the water lilies. The diversity of ecosystems found in this region – coastal, rainforest woodland and open savannah – provides a habitat for many large and exotic species. For serious birders, far north Queensland is one of the most productive and rewarding parts of the planet.

A slightly longer journey would take you into the Torres Strait Islands, the honeyed islands that form stepping stones between Australia with Papua New Guinea, each one trimmed with a narrow fringe of sugar-white sand that dissolves toward a peacock-blue sea teeming with corals and exotic marine life.

If time and budget allow, there's also the option of a journey west across the Top End, which would include such wonders as the Gulf of Carpentaria, the miraculous wetlands and the harsh stone country of Arnhem Land and the Kimberley coast, one of Australia's unsung heavens.

Barmaga
Shelburne
Bay
*Cape York
Peninsula*
Weipa
Princess
Charlotte
Bay
Coen
Cooktown
*Gulf of
Carpentaria*
Cairns
QUEENSLAND

CAPE YORK HELICOPTER SAFARIS

LOCATION: Tours usually begin and end in Cairns but other departure points are available.

GETTING THERE: Qantas, Virgin Blue and Australian Airlines fly into Cairns.

WHAT'S INCLUDED: Apart from incidental expenses along the way, tours with Cape York Helicopter Safaris are normally all-inclusive.

MAKING THE MOST OF IT: Pack light, but take clothing that can be layered to suit varying conditions. Take plenty of film and all-purpose footwear.

CONTACT: Outback Encounter
33 Queen Street, Thebarton
South Australia, 5031, Australia
Telephone + 61 8 **8354 4405**
Facsimile + 61 8 **8354 4406**
Email info@outbackencounter.com
Website www.outbackencounter.com

REEF ENCOUNTER

What could be better than diving in one of the world's natural wonders? Try travelling and staying there on a boat of pure luxury.

The Great Barrier Reef, where feeding the fish
takes on a whole new meaning.

Reef Encounter provides a
window to the treasures
of one of the world's
natural wonders.

IT'S NO SECRET that Australia has sensational scuba diving. There are many reasons, including a healthy marine environment, a huge diversity of underwater conditions, warm seas, a vast array of sea life and a natural passion for the sea. For anyone new to the sport, Australia is one of the best places to train as a certified diver, with the assurance that Australian diving operations are professionally run and equipment is well maintained.

There's also Queensland's Great Barrier Reef, the world's largest reef system and one of the seven natural wonders off the world – an awesome total of more than 2800 individual reefs stretching for more than 2000 kilometres along the east coast. The Great Barrier Reef also forms a bulwark against the Pacific Ocean. Inside this breakwater is a 250,000-square-kilometre maritime province – a vast labyrinth of smaller reefs, coral cays, lagoons, rocky inshore islands, deep channels and underwater caverns. In these warm, shallow waters nature has run riot and created a vast, chaotic profusion of marine life. The greatest concentration of natural splendours is found on the outer reef, where the nutrient-rich sea fosters a vast profusion of marine life that few other places can match.

While there is no shortage of vessels that make day-trips out to the reef from Cairns and Port Douglas, if you want to experience the full array of wonders that the Great Barrier Reef offers – whether you have just 24 hours or a week to spare – you can't do better than *Reef Encounter*. Moored on the Outer Reef just off the city of Cairns, this striking, 35-metre vessel is operated by a young, energetic and professional crew.

Access to *Reef Encounter* is either a two-hour boat ride from Cairns or a brief, spectacular helicopter flight. If time is important, the chopper is the way to go, and there are few experiences more thrilling than the sea eagle's-eye view of coral reefs, complete with pods of dolphins, whales and even turtles if the sea is calm.

Depending on the weather, the vessel may relocate several times during the day to another section of reef. Even a fairly short journey will usher you into a whole new underwater world of reefs waiting to be explored.

Apart from its journeys along the Great Barrier Reef, *Reef Encounter* is also available for charter work throughout the region. The vessel's long-range fuel tanks and desalination capacity gives her the ability to take passengers and crew far off the beaten track. In fact, the only real limits are your imagination. Among the options are the rugged Kimberley coastline, Papua New Guinea and, closer at hand, the glorious tropical islands of Torres Strait.

For most visitors though, the spectacle of the Great Barrier Reef is more than enough. Miss out on this and you miss one of the greatest experiences Australia has to offer.

Surrounded by a pristine world of corals and sea life, *Reef Encounter* allows you to relax in style at the end of the day.

Reef Encounter provides an all-encompassing aquatic experience for her guests.

THE FACILITIES ON board the fully airconditioned vessel are great. On the top deck, the two deluxe staterooms are modern, spacious and bright with plenty of storage space. Like the other staterooms on the upper and middle decks, each has an ensuite bathroom. *Reef Encounter* also makes all her own water via a big desalination plant and guests have the luxury of unlimited showers. The dining room is big and fresh, and close to the bow of the vessel is a big spa bath – perfect for watching the sunset with a glass of champagne.

Three times a day meals are served in the ship's diningroom, each one calculated to satisfy a healthy appetite that comes with a day of healthy outdoor activity. There's also a bar, and tea and coffee are available throughout the day.

IT'S ALL ABOUT the sea – and in these surroundings, that's only natural. Dive sessions begin at first light, and there are opportunities to dive several times during each day, as well as night diving after dinner. And since most dive sites on the Great Barrier Reef are fairly shallow, it's no problem to fit in several dives per day without exceeding decompression times.

At the stern of the vessel, a hydraulic platform makes diving and snorkelling a breeze. When *Reef Encounter* is anchored, the platform is sunk to surface level to make for easy water entry and exit. When it's time to board the dive boat to access a more distant location, the boat is lifted to deck level on the platform to make it easily accessible for divers.

For divers who have already completed an open-water course, the divemaster on board can help hone your skills with night-diving or navigation courses. For novices who have never dived before, this is the perfect introduction. The water is warm, the visibility is exceptional, and you'll never have a more exciting entrée to the underwater world than this. The on-board dive instructor will fit you out with a wetsuit, a buoyancy compensator jacket, weight belt and mask, explain the mysteries of atmospheric pressure, soothe your fears and usher you safely below. The initial dive lasts for about 30 minutes and descends to a depth of about nine metres. Divers can also study to complete their SSI Open Water Dive Course on board the vessel, and there's no better place to learn than here, with the ultimate swimming pool all around you.

It isn't really necessary to dive to experience the natural wonders of the Great Barrier Reef. At low tide, when the coral formations are close to the surface, all you have to do is slip on a face mask, snorkel and fins and loiter around on the surface and you'll experience a wealth of darting, shimmering, multi-coloured marine life.

Take a dive – whether you're an accomplished diver or a complete novice – and experience one of the world's great underwater treasures.

REEF ENCOUNTER

LOCATION: On the Great Barrier Reef, off the city of Cairns.

GETTING THERE: Either by helicopter or boat transfer from Cairns.

WHAT'S INCLUDED: All meals and snorkelling activities. Dive packages on the *Reef Encounter* are an economical way to go.

MAKING THE MOST OF IT: Sun protection is a must, and non-slip footwear that's easy to get on and off and doesn't mind water.

CONTACT: Outback Encounter
33 Queen Street, Thebarton
South Australia, 5031, Australia
Telephone + 61 8 **8354 4405**
Facsimile + 61 8 **8354 4406**
Email info@outbackencounter.com
Website www.outbackencounter.com

SPICERS PEAK LODGE
SCENIC RIM

Hidden in the ranges of south-east Queensland lies a retreat comparable to the best small hotels of Europe or North America.

CHISELLED FROM THE rugged forests of the Main Range to the west of Brisbane, in south-east Queensland, this is an unsuspected treasure – a marvellous country house in pristine surroundings with chic and urbane tastes in food and lodging; the very best of both worlds. This is an exclusive retreat, a quieter alternative to the brashness of the Gold Coast, which lies a 90-minute drive to the east, blessed with cool summers and mild winters that make this a prime choice for the adventurous traveller who revels in the great outdoors.

Spicers Peak does not reveal itself lightly. Just after the Cunningham Highway spirals into the heights of the Main Range National Park, just over an hour's drive west of Brisbane, a gravel road turns into the hills and commences a meandering journey through the paddocks. It begins mildly enough, skittering through pastures and thick forests of eucalypts, but then the road becomes a narrow ramp, the trees lock arms overhead and the journey enters another dimension. Wallabies bound across the road and cattle watch as you splash across little streams with a knowing nod of their heads. Grass trees appear by the roadside – huge, shaggy clumps of fibres on the end of stubby trunks. Despite the signs, you're beginning to wonder if you're on the right track when, finally, the dense woodland clears at a hilltop and crowning the summit is the sturdy, refined profile of Spicers Peak Lodge.

The lodge is baronial in scale. Pull up at the porte cochere in the circular drive, step inside and you're in a handsome and beautifully-appointed loungeroom with imperial dimensions that manages to dwarf the baby grand piano in the corner. On the far side of the room, the view of pastures dotted with Black Angus cattle and forested hills is framed by enormous timber beams.

Despite its scale, the mood is intimate and club-like. Couches and comfortable armchairs divide the lounge room into smaller rooms, and there are books and magazines close at hand. The colours are a rich blend of chocolate and coffee, with an occasional scoop of vanilla. Chiselled into a wooden beam above the fireplace is a Latin inscription, which translates as, 'The best and most beautiful support in life is friendship'. One floor above is a billiard table and a catwalk that leads to an observation deck.

Spicers Peak opened at Easter, 2004, yet by incorporating a wealth of historic detail in the construction, it suggests a far longer lineage. The fireplace that dominates the loungeroom as well as many of the walls are made from blocks of dark stone that were imported from Scotland as ballast in sailing ships, and once used to build warehouses along the wharves in Port Adelaide. The timber uprights that soar the top of the mezzanine floor are made from steel clad with aged timber, yet the deception is skilled and convincing.

During your stay you'll discover that Spicers Peak elevates good living to an art form. It also comes with a repertoire of brisk, outdoor pleasures – especially for those who enjoy bushwalking. The ingredients that make up Spicers Peak – the lorikeets that descend on the lawn each morning, the views of pastures and cattle and rippling hills, the crash of wallabies hurtling through the bush – are all special in their own way. Combined with the panache, the sophistication and the level of service that Spicers Peak brings to the equation, these natural flavours elevate this to a property of distinction. ⬂

Crisp, refined, relaxed – all the good adjectives apply at this oasis of style and good living.

This a prime choice for the traveller who revels in the great outdoors.

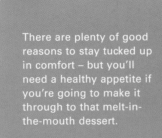
There are plenty of good reasons to stay tucked up in comfort – but you'll need a healthy appetite if you're going to make it through to that melt-in-the-mouth dessert.

THERE ARE JUST 10 guest rooms, and they're all beautiful. Most have fireplaces, made from the same stone ballast blocks that were imported from Scotland. The ensuite bathrooms are enormous, and stocked with a range of L'Occitane bath products. In the spa rooms, the circular spa bath is set beneath a glass roof. Rooms have interior shutters on the windows and double doors that open to a verandah where you can watch the grazing cows. There's also a day bed on a banquette beneath the windows and every room has a king-size bed.

The meals at Spicers Peak are nothing less than sensational. A team of skilled chefs works wonders in the kitchen to produce inventive cuisine that takes the palate on a journey though the best of modern Australian food. Breakfast is a choice of cereals, yoghurt, fruit and bread, as well as an à la carte menu, which might offer prosciutto, asparagus, tomato and fontina cheese served on a polenta cake, or buttermilk pancakes with maple syrup and crumbled honeycomb with a dollop of ricotta.

Lunch might begin with bruschetta with caramelised onion, Persian fetta and wild rocket, followed by grilled swordfish with salad nicoise and grilled lemon. Dinner is a degustation menu which might begin with a Thai-style prawn soup, followed by a tartlet with onion and prosciutto, then a mandarin sorbet followed by a chunk of salmon served on a crisp rosti with asparagus, then a confit of duck with a sweet potato purée, poached tamarillo and spinach.

Dessert might be a chocolate and pistachio semi freddo between a sandwich of honey wafers. Wines are served throughout the meal designed to complement each course. This is not a menu to be taken lightly. It pays to plan an energetic day to appreciate food of this calibre. The chef can also prepare a gourmet picnic lunch at Ryan's Lookout, about a 20-minute walk from the lodge, which is set high on a hillside above a plummeting valley. All meals and drinks are included in the tariff.

Whet your appetite – food just doesn't get better than this.

Walk, bike, hike and partake –
then be pampered by your
choice of massage therapy.

THE CARPET OF hills and forests that unfolds from the lodge is one to stir lungs and legs to action, and the region comes with a full-blooded array of things to do. Spicers Peak is surrounded by the Main Range National Park, which boasts natural majesty and beauty that have ensured its inclusion on the list of Australia's World Heritage zones. The rich, volcanic soil supports a wide array of forest types that provide the backdrop for a number of wilderness adventures, including bushwalks and mountain-biking, and the lodge has 24-speed Scott MTBs with front suspension plus helmets and gloves.

The 9000-acre property is laced with bushwalking trails that present varying challenges, and staff at the lodge can supply maps and advice. The lodge can also arrange four-wheel-drive tours of the property. In the immediate area are several other areas of outstanding beauty, many of which contain significant areas of rainforest, luscious green gardens filled with rioting vegetation and exotic birds and animals.

As well as the heated pool at the front of the lodge, there's also a hardcourt tennis court off to one side. Massage therapies are available by prior arrangement. The lodge has access to a skilled practitioner in Reiki and Swedish massage and reflexology and aromatherapy – the perfect end to a day spent out on the trail. There's also a mob of Highland cattle that are always delighted to see human company, especially when they come with carrots in their hands.

Pedal the wild ranges, lock horns with the local wildlife, but whatever you do, carpe diem!

SPICERS PEAK LODGE SCENIC RIM

LOCATION: About 130 kilometres west of Brisbane.

GETTING THERE: The drive from Brisbane takes about 90 minutes. The final 12 kilometres is along a torturous track that requires caution. You can charter a helicopter for an exhilarating 30-minute flight across the ranges.

WHAT'S INCLUDED: All meals and drinks and activities.

MAKING THE MOST OF IT: Take walking shoes and sun protection. Winters are mild and sunny.

CONTACT: Outback Encounter
33 Queen Street, Thebarton
South Australia, 5031, Australia
Telephone + 61 8 **8354 4405**
Facsimile + 61 8 **8354 4406**
Email info@outbackencounter.com
Website www.outbackencounter.com

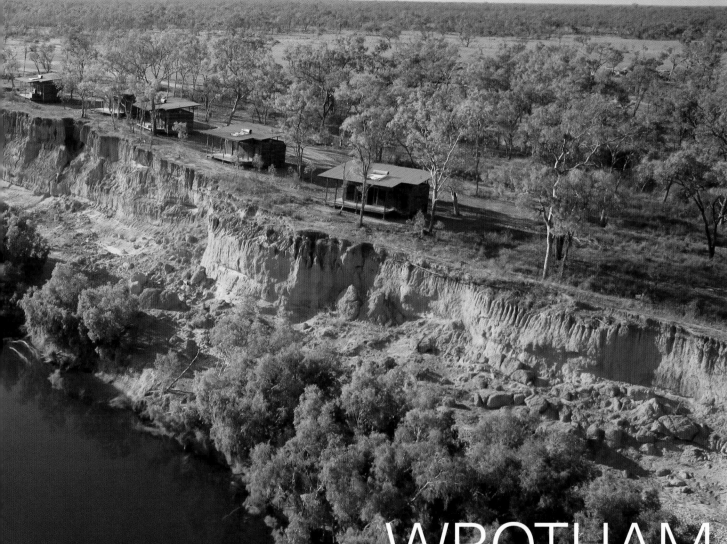

WROTHAM PARK LODGE

Poised above a deep river gorge, this luxury retreat brings a high-gloss finish to the outback cattle station experience.

Among the many unique attractions that Australia has to offer, the cattle station stands out.

IF YOU WANT to sample the essence of outback Australia and the remarkable people who live there, there's nothing like a spell on a cattle station, and this striking, handsome lodge brings serenity and a consummate sense of style to the cattle station experience.

Set dramatically on a gorge overlooking the Mitchell River in north Queensland, Wrotham Park Lodge was inspired by the vernacular forms of Australian bush architecture. Roofs are corrugated iron, the timber cladding is rough and raw, verandahs are furnished with "squatter" chairs, with leg rests that swing out to accommodate feet tired out from a day in the stirrups – but the comfort level is set to maximum. The big deck at the front of the homestead has a wet-edge pool that mirrors the sky, there's an air-conditioned lounge with books and a plasma TV and a well-stocked open bar, and at the end of every canoe trip or station drive, a smiling staff member

appears with an iced towel scented with Wrotham's signature oil.

The scenery is heart-stopping. Just a few metres from the homestead is a mighty gulf that the Mitchell River has gnawed from the bank, and which has been sculpted by the elements. This "lost city" of spire and pinnacles is a source of wonder and fascination, one that changes constantly as the sun moves across the sky. For most of the year the Mitchell River is a languid brown snake, coiling lazily through the casuarinas along its banks, but during the wet season between December and March, it rises into a foaming, raging dynamo. The distance from the lip of the chasm at your feet to the far bank is half a kilometre in most places at least, which gives an idea of the river's power to rearrange this tobacco-coloured landscape.

Birds feature prominently in the region's wildlife. Kingfishers and kookaburras are common

The homestead stands out as an oasis of refinement and good living amid the spectacularly rugged surroundings and the daily workings of Wrotham Park Station, a 660,000-hectare working cattle station.

along the riverbanks and if you glance up to the sky from your sun lounge there are kites and wedge-tailed eagles hovering overhead. Travel just a short distance from the lodge and you'll come across pairs of sarus cranes – the world's tallest flying bird – stalking across the biscuit-coloured plains. On MacKenzie's Lagoon, whistling ducks and magpie geese riot and honk among the water lilies, and there are usually jacanas – also known as the "Jesus" bird because it appears to walk on water – stalking across the lily pads.

The open plains are home to eastern grey kangaroos, which can be seen grazing on grasslands during the cool of early morning and evening. If you're lucky, you might spot a freshwater crocodile along the river, and although the name might send shivers down your spine, these shy, narrow-snouted reptiles are relatively harmless compared with the "salty" – the aggressive estuarine crocodile.

A wealth of well-tailored detail wherever you look.

FOOD IS ONE of the highlights at Wrotham Park Resort, from the breakfast of eggs with smoked salmon and espresso to the warm scones with silky cream and homemade preserves that appear in the afternoon. Served in the breezy dining room, dinners bring a light, sophisticated touch inspired by the flavours of the Mediterranean to local ingredients such as kangaroo and barramundi – both prominent on the table d'hote dinner menu.

One of the specialties is 1824 beef, which is produced by the Australian Agricultural Company, Australia's largest beef producer and the owner of Wrotham Park Station. Available in some of Australia' best restaurants, the 1824 brand is rapidly acquiring a fine reputation for its flavour and tenderness. All meals are included in the tariff, and so are all the drinks from the well-stocked bar.

Set among the trees along the riverbank, the 10 air-conditioned guest bungalows – "Quarters" – elevate rusticity to an art form. Inside each is a smart, soothing enclave decorated and furnished from a subdued palette of chocolate and taupe, with big grey floor tiles. One side of the shower is a floor-to-ceiling window that frames a view of eucalypts and the trough of the Mitchell River.

At the front of each of the quarters is a broad verandah with a day bed, just the place for listening to the birds.

Earth-toned rooms are chic, minimalist and subdued, and the contemporary tone flows through into the dining room, where every meal is a celebration.

The waterways provide a wealth of opportunities for fishing or canoeing – or you can take to the air with a muster pilot, learn how to crack a bullwhip, or just sit back on the deck and wait for sunset.

WROTHAM PARK STATION RESORT
- Mouth Organ Yards
- Wrotham Park Stn
- Mitchell River
- Burke Developmental Road
- QUEENSLAND
- Chillagoe
- Dimbulah
- Mareeba
- Cairns

Bringing style and serenity to the outback cattle station experience.

ALTHOUGH THE SCENERY, the sun lounges and the swimming pool can keep you happily engaged for hours, Wrotham Park cries out for exploration. Canoes are available for paddling along the Mitchell River, with an expert guide ready to show you the best fishing spots. There are also mountain bikes if you feel the urge to saddle up, and the chef can arrange a gourmet riverside picnic.

The best reason to come to Wrotham Park, though, is the chance to experience life, work and play on an outback cattle station. At the heart of 6000-square kilometre property – almost twice the size of the King Ranch in Texas - is a small and largely self-sufficient community of mechanics, cooks, drovers and chopper pilots who manage 35,000 Brahman cattle.

Although they might sleep in airconditioned quarters these days and check their email every couple of days, these are men and women who nourish the essential bush skills of ingenuity, independence and a wry sense of humour.

Novice station workers – jackaroos and jillaroos – must still break in the horses they will use to muster cattle on the thirsty plains of Wrotham Park, and any one of them can show you how to crack a whip with a sound like a gunshot. Take the time to share their lives and you'll come away with special memories of a special place.

WROTHAM PARK LODGE

LOCATION: 330 kilometres west of Cairns, it's about a four-hour drive or 45-minute flight.

GETTING THERE: Scheduled flights by twin-engine aircraft operate between Cairns and Wrotham Park on Monday, Wednesday and Friday. Charter flights can be arranged on other days or for large groups.

WHAT'S INCLUDED: All meals and guided activities.

MAKING THE MOST OF IT: Expect hot, dusty conditions, but nights can be cool in mid-year. Take sturdy footwear and a broad-brimmed hat.

CONTACT: Outback Encounter
33 Queen Street, Thebarton
South Australia, 5031, Australia
Telephone + 61 8 **8354 4405**
Facsimile + 61 8 **8354 4406**
Email info@outbackencounter.com
Website www.outbackencounter.com

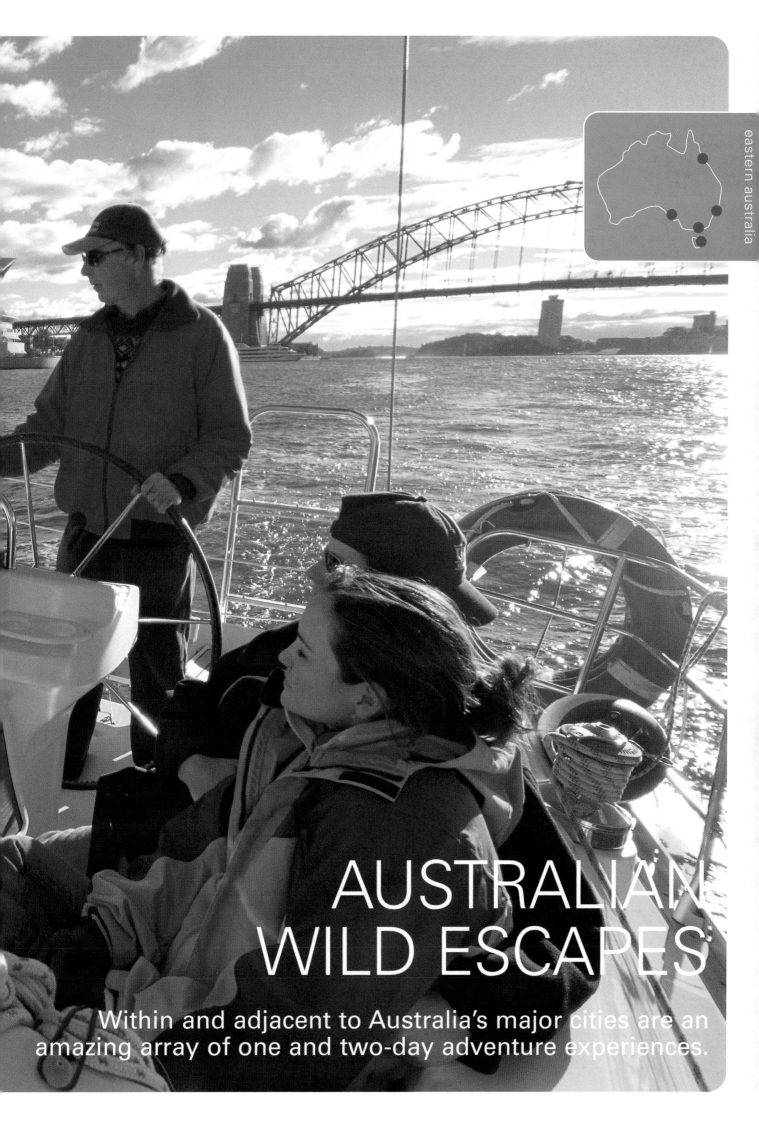

AUSTRALIAN WILD ESCAPES

Within and adjacent to Australia's major cities are an amazing array of one and two-day adventure experiences.

Despite its glamour, Sydney also has its quiet harbourside villages, and a Wild Escapes guide can let you in on the secrets.

Unravel the secrets of our cities with a convivial friend who knows how to lay on a superb lunch at a great location.

AUSTRALIA'S CITIES are among the country's prime attractions. When asked to nominate their favourite city, for the past several years world travellers have placed Sydney at the top of the list. Melbourne is also ranks highly – a cosmopolitan, cultivated city with its own unique style, while Adelaide and Hobart are historic jewels, splendidly endowed with buildings dating back to the earliest days of settlement.

Unravelling the secrets of these cities is not so easy, particularly if time is limited. Melbourne and Sydney are huge metropolises, with populations of three to four million, and they're far from compact. As anyone will tell you, just navigating Sydney's road system is enough to make even most Australians call the nearest cab. If you want to make the most of your time in Australia's cities, you're going to need an expert to show you around the sights, and there is nobody better than Australian Wild Escapes.

From its beginnings as an ecotourism operator, Australian Wild Escapes has had almost 20 years expertise in introducing visitors to the best Australia has to offer – cities, wineries, beaches, scenic splendours and wildlife. What's more, they'll serve the experience with style, from the plush, well-appointed tour vehicle that picks you up from your hotel to the well-chilled wine accompanying lunch. When you tour Sydney Harbour, for example, you'll be aboard a private yacht where you can help with the ropes and take

the wheel if you feel like it – not one of the giant tour boats that lumber around the harbour with several hundred tourists on board.

With bases in Sydney, Melbourne, Adelaide, Hobart and Cairns, Wild Escapes is well equipped to show you around – whether it's a misty, tangled, tropical rainforest, the glamorous beaches that line Sydney's Pacific coast or the chill ruins of the convict-built settlement at Tasmania's Port Arthur.

If you want a tour that's even more out of the ordinary, Wild Escapes has just the thing. For an unforgettable view of the harbour city, what about a helicopter flight from Sydney to the Blue Mountains, followed by a tour of the region's stunning sandstone chasms and a leisurely drive back to your hotel? Or perhaps a seaplane flight over Sydney Harbour, combined with a tour of Kur-ring-Gai National Park, the rugged bushland to the north? There's also a range of more intense experiences under the label "Australia's Best Kept Secrets" – two-day trips to areas of exceptional natural beauty from Sydney, Melbourne, Hobart and Cairns, with five-star accommodation along the way.

It's also friendly. In fact, many liken a tour with Wild Escapes to the experience of exploring a city with a convivial friend who knows all its secrets, who's also a great raconteur and who knows how to lay on a superb lunch at a great location.

Ancient stones, modern marvels and bushland rambles – Wild Escapes will help you make the most of your holiday time in Australia's stunning cities.

Even in Sydney, you can avoid the madding crowd soak up the views and enjoy the sights in peace.

A TYPICAL DAY with Australian Wild Escapes begins with a pickup from your city hotel. Your vehicle will depend on the tour you've chosen – but it might be anything from a luxury people mover to a rugged four-wheel-drive. Whichever vehicle is provided, you're assured of comfort, space, security and a fabulous view. But what really sets Australian Wild Escapes apart more than any other factor is its tour guides. Friendly, authoritative and enthusiastic, they have a depth of knowledge that takes a Wild Escapes tour to a new level. On the tour of the Blue Mountains west of Sydney, for example, instead of the view of the Three Sisters from Echo Point – always crowded with sightseers – your Australian Wild Escapes guide will take you to a secluded spot further along the cliffs where you won't have to compete with the hordes for a breathtaking view. Along the way, they'll use the sights as triggers to delve into Australia's history and contemporary society – which might be anything from the latest political scandal to the price of Sydney's waterfront real estate. These guides are also expert naturalists who can tell you about the reproduction cycle of the kangaroo, the strategies that eucalyptus trees use to conserve water or the feeding habits of the fairy penguin.

Come lunchtime and the guides put on a chef's hat and serve up a fine barbeque at a secluded bush location – or take you to a beachside picnic spot for fish and chips with a prime view over Sydney Harbour.

Wildlife parks give tour participants the chance to get a close look at the local fauna. A day trip to the Blue Mountains is a wonderful escape out of Sydney, while the city itself offers icon views at almost every turn.

EACH CITY HAS has its own distinct appeal. Sydney is big, brash and beautiful, with the most expensive real estate in the country, the busiest streets and the raunchiest nightlife of any Australian city. Melbourne is a more tranquil city that prides itself on its European flavour, and the city has a wonderful array of dining and entertainment. Close to the city are two jewels that no visitor should miss – the towering forests of the Dandenong Ranges and the Yarra Valley, a premium winegrowing district.

Spacious and gracious, Adelaide is a charming city built along the banks of a lazy river, with its own distinctive bluestone architecture. Adelaide is also the gateway to the Barossa Valley, Australia's most illustrious winegrowing region. Cairns is a beauty, the entrée to the tropical glories of the north Queensland rainforests and the Great Barrier Reef, and a city richly-endowed with great hotels and dining and shopping galore.

Hobart is compact and charming, a city brimming with history, from the stone warehouses along its waterfront to the twisting streets of Battery Point that overlook the harbour. These cities are also a great place to get acquainted with Australia's unique fauna. While there's nothing to compare with the experience of watching a kangaroo bounding across a grassy plain or seeing the flash of wings of a rainbow lorikeet through the trees, much of Australia's wildlife is elusive.

Many Australians will go their whole lives without ever seeing a platypus in the wild – yet each city has wildlife parks where you can get a close up look at these animals in an environment that is as close to its natural habitat as possible, and Australian Wild Escapes will take you right to where the action is.

Adjacent to the 'big smoke' you'll be amazed at what each hinterland and coastline has to offer.

OUTBACK
ENCOUNTER
PORTFOLIO
MEMBER

AUSTRALIAN WILD ESCAPES

LOCATION: Australian Wild Escapes operate tours from offices in Sydney, Melbourne, Adelaide, Hobart and Cairns.

WHAT'S INCLUDED: Pick-up from accommodation, all admission fees, lunch and snacks.

MAKING THE MOST OF IT: All you need is a camera. For clothing and footwear recommendations, contact the Wild Escapes office organising your tour.

CONTACT: Outback Encounter
33 Queen Street, Thebarton
South Australia, 5031, Australia
Telephone + 61 8 **8354 4405**
Facsimile + 61 8 **8354 4406**
Email info@outbackencounter.com
Website www.outbackencounter.com

BURRAWANG WEST STATION

Sublime accommodation on a central-western
New South Wales cattle station brings a fresh twist
to the sturdy traditions of the bush.

The classic traditions of colonial Australia
come together with stunning success.

AT BURRAWANG WEST Station, the experience is presented luxuriously, in stirring surroundings with a potent sense of tradition and an appreciation for style, design and good living that is rarely seen.

This is still a proud and self-reliant world, where the old-fashioned traditions of warmth, practicality and hospitality are honoured as nowhere else.

Set on the outskirts of Parkes on the plains of the Central West of New South Wales, Burrawang West was established in Australia's pioneering era of the 1830s. By the late 1800s, when Burrawang ran more than 273,000 sheep spread across 227,000 hectares, it operated one of the largest shearing sheds in Australia, employing more than 250 men. In the 1990s, Burrawang was acquired by a Japanese corporation as an Australian bush retreat for its executives. The concept was lavish.

Responsibility for the design went to Denton Corker Marshall, one of Australia's most fashionable and prestigious architects. From the huge cedar doors that were specially crafted for the interior to the mesh-covered cabinets that were specially designed for the kitchens, the craftsmanship as well as the execution is meticulous, a tribute to the skills of the architects as well as the builders. When the corporation downsized its Australian operations, the property was acquired by its present owner, who decided to open it as an upscale retreat for a lucky few.

Burrawang West takes its inspiration from the classic traditions of colonial Australia. The homestead is a long, low, timber building surrounded by a broad verandah. The entrance hallway leads to an expansive formal drawing room with well-padded sofas and a baby grand piano. French doors open to the verandah and wide-angle views across the lawns to the thick belt of timber that screens the billabong. At one side of the sitting room is a bar and billiards room and on the other, a formal dining room.

Although the house is aristocratic in character, it is essentially a modern eclectic work, marrying antique walnut tables with citrus-coloured walls

The architecture takes
its inspiration from the
vernacular forms
of the Australian bush.
The homestead brings
poise and elegance to
the thirsty western
plains of NSW.

and bold geometric fabrics on the armchairs and cushions in the billiard room.

Throughout, the homestead and the bungalows are decorated with artworks that show a fine sensitivity to contemporary nuances. This is a highly individualistic and self-confident assembly of Australian art that blends naïve art of the colonial period with botanical lithographs, powerful contemporary sculptures and folk art samplers and quilts.

Burrawang's Aboriginal artwork includes two striking works, one in the dot painting style of Yuendumu, one of the wellsprings of art in the Central Desert region, the other a fine bark painting by Mick Gubargu, one of the finest bark painters.

In the hallway of the homestead, a kimono splayed on the wall in metal plates hints at the Japanese connection, while walls in the retreats are decorated with cross-cut saws and scythes that strike a powerful reminder of the muscular contribution of Australia's pioneers.

Accommodation that derives its elegance from pure functionality and a fine sense of proportion.

THIS IS COUNTRY cooking at its finest. All food and drinks are included in the tariff, and from breakfast to dinner, there is much to savour. Many of the ingredients are sourced from the immediate surrounds, either from the vegetable garden or from the pastures of the 10,000-acre property.

Burrawang Beef is a distinctive and well-recognised label, produced from the Angus, Simmental and Shorthorn-cross cattle raised on Burrawang's specially-sown pastures to produce beef of outstanding flavour and tenderness. There is no better place to sample this superb beef, whether it's served at the antique dining table or in the less formal surrounds of a poolside barbecue.

As well as meals, all drinks are included, and the wine cellar is a collection of some of the finest Australian labels. There's also an open bar, located in the club-like surrounds of the billiard room.

Guest accommodation is located in the four retreats – the cottages that lie scattered between the homestead and the billabong – and the screened verandahs and weathered timber cladding gives no hint of the luxuries within. Inside each is a large, luxurious enclave with gleaming timber floors and high ceilings.

Each retreat has two bedrooms separated by a big common lounge room, and each bedroom has its own ensuite bathroom with a clawfoot bath and shower. Furnishings such as the chests of drawers and wardrobes in the bedrooms have an almost Shaker-like simplicity, an elegance derived from pure functionality and a fine sense of proportion.

The retreats have reverse-cycle air conditioning for year-round comfort, but there's also a fireplace for winter nights and chopped firewood on the verandah.

The artfulness of Burrawang's design lies is its simplicity, accented by a taste for the finer things in life. The façade of the homestead is a satisfying composition straight from the classical mould.

ACTIVITIES

From stargazing through the telescope on the star viewing platform to zooming across the paddocks on a quad bike to paddling on the billabong, Burrawang is packed with surprises.

Time to play? Burrawang dishes up a feast for those who want to experience bush life.

ALTHOUGH BURRAWANG TODAY is only a fraction of the original quarter-million hectare holding, the property retains all the apparatus of the grazing empire it once was. Scattered across the property are shearing sheds, cottages and barns, some of which date from the 1800s.

For guests, one of the highlights is touring the property on a quad bike, and after a quick lesson just about anyone can pilot one of these all-terrain vehicles with ease. One of the loveliest drives is along the track that winds beside the billabong, where kangaroos frequently graze beneath the paperbarks.

When it comes time to play, Burrawang is comprehensively equipped. Off to one side of the homestead, screened by a large, coniferous hedge and a formal rose garden, there's a 20-metre heated swimming pool and spa pool. Set slightly apart in a country cottage is The Clubhouse, which has saunas, spas, showers and storeroom for the archery equipment and golf clubs for the driving range. Completing this line-up of sporting excellence are two floodlit all-weather tennis courts. On the far side of the rambling lawns below the house, the Boatshed has canoes, fishing gear and easy access to Yarrabandai Billabong, a prime spot for birdwatching.

One of the most striking features of the property is the telescope which sits on top of the three-storey Star Viewing Platform in the lawn at the front of the homestead. The skies here are well known for their clarity and lack of pollution, which is the reason that nearby Parkes was chosen as the site for Australia's radio telescope. Even for novice stargazers, the sheer abundance of the night sky here is unforgettable.

Dubbo

Condobolin

Lake
Cargelligo

Parkes

BURRAWANG

Forbes

Cowra

Mid Western
Highway

West
Wyalong

Grenfell

Newell Highway

N E W   S O U T H   W A L E S

BURRAWANG WEST STATION

LOCATION: 435 kilometres west of Sydney. From Parkes Airport, it's a one-hour drive.

GETTING THERE: Best option is a flight, the drive is long and tiring.

WHAT'S INCLUDED: All meals, drinks and activities.

MAKING THE MOST OF IT: Days are generally warm to hot, but nights can be cool. Take sturdy footwear that offers protection from the dust. Elastic-sided boots are ideal.

CONTACT: Outback Encounter
33 Queen Street, Thebarton
South Australia, 5031, Australia
Telephone + 61 8 **8354 4405**
Facsimile + 61 8 **8354 4406**
Email info@outbackencounter.com
Website www.outbackencounter.com

BOATSHED

THE BYRON AT BYRON RESORT

Byron Bay is a shimmering jewel that attracts hedonists from around the world – and now there's another reason to go.

A beautiful resort equipped for leisure and pleasure in the heart of Byron Bay.

BYRON BAY ON the north coast of New South Wales occupies the most easterly point on the Australian mainland. The lighthouse at the southern end of the town is also the brightest lighthouse in the country, and if you're looking for symbolism, this is exactly where it should be. Byron Bay has star quality. Its natural credentials are impeccable. Beaches the rest of the world would kill for, there's sunshine galore, dolphins ride the breaking waves below the lighthouse, storms hang rainbows on the high peaks of the hinterland – yes, Byron Bay has an aura, and it casts its spell over practically everyone who goes there.

It is only fitting, therefore, that one of Australia's newest and most glamorous resorts, The Byron at Byron, also belongs here. Created in what was once a neglected paperbark wetland on a 18-hectare site about a five-minute drive south of the town centre, this is a beautiful resort. At its core is a sweeping verandah that houses the reception area, the gym, spa and restaurant. On the far side of the main building is a giant swimming pool arranged with sculptural compositions of deck chairs.

On the far side is a solid wall of wetland forest, where boardwalks wind through the bangalow palms and into paperbarks and ponds where spoonbills stalk though the shallows. The boardwalk ends at Tallow Lake, and beyond is the beach of the same name, one of the many sensational beaches in this part of the world.

Presiding over The Byron at Byron is a pair of vastly experienced hoteliers, John and Lyn Parche, who have infused the resort with their warmth, vision and style. "We want this to be your living room," says Lyn, sweeping her arm to embrace the foyer, the outdoor seating on the deck and the restaurant. The details are exquisite. There are petals floating in the narrow channels of the decorative ponds and dramatic flower arrangements everywhere. The resort is also comprehensively equipped for leisure and pleasure. The heated swimming pool is huge, and the spa offers a wide array of massages, naturopathy treatments, body wraps and facials.

While The Byron at Byron offers plenty of reasons to venture no further than the reception desk, this is an area that repays exploration. The town has a lively array of adventure sports, from scuba diving to sky diving. The beaches are some of Australia's best, and casting its psychic shadow over Byron Bay is a hinterland of lush, green, volcanic hills that has been tamed into macadamia farms and banana plantations, or left to run feral in World Heritage National Parks.

The Byron at Byron Resort brings a silk touch to one of the country's funkiest coastal towns.

The food at Wild at Byron is exceptional, using local and regional produce and showing them off in serene surroundings. And for overnight guests, the luxurious suites offer quality at every turn.

A statement of class and style that blends perfectly into an environment to envy.

GUEST ROOMS ARE located in two-storey wings that wander into the forest on either side of the main lodge building – and they're a real surprise. Instead of the low-rise, camouflage green that you might expect of a resort that prides itself on its eco credentials, there are bold and sculptural, arranged in two storeys and framed by orange steel joists. Black screens provide insect proofing and steel mesh glitters on the side of the metal staircases. Inside, the suites are sensational. The front door opens to a screened verandah which is followed by a big lounge room with kitchen facilities and a big couch opposite a plasma TV screen. Opaque glass screens slide across to separate the lounge room from the bathroom and bedroom, which are connected via a walk-through wardrobe. There's quality in every department here, from the smooth linen on the king-size bed to the huge free-standing bath to the lighting – probably the best you'll find in a resort room anywhere. The mood is cool and relaxed, the powder-blue couch and the bed cushions striking contrasting note to the blonde timbers and white walls.

The resort's restaurant, Wild at Byron, is seriously fantastic. Chefs Matthew Wild and Gavin Hughes have come up with a menu that celebrate the changing produce that each new season brings. The spring menu might feature entrees such as char grilled Yamba prawns with a braise or tomato, fennel and olives, or a pork terrine with prunes and Armagnac jelly. Main courses might be clay baked snapper with sweet potato and preserved lemon, a paella or a classic bouillabaisse.

Ably assisted by their skilled staff, John and Lyn Parche offer a lesson in the art of good living.

New-age, old-age, any age – the word Byron alone conjures up images of life's best indulgences.

JUST POKING AROUND the shops at Byron Bay or people watching at one of the outdoor cafes provides endless fascination. Wholefood, hippiedom, handcrafted and back-to-nature prevail. Whether you want a dawn yoga session on the beach, a reiki massage, an aura refurbishment, a chakra realignment or a complete spiritual rebirthing, Byron Bay is the place to go. The town's lighthouse is the first point on the coast to feel the glow of the morning sun, and a lovely walking track winds around the lighthouse to the rocks below.

The beaches at Byron Bay – Main, Watego's, the great sweep of Tallow – are just about everything anyone could ask for in the sun, sand and sea department. For a quieter alternative, head south to Broken Bay Reserve, a jaw-dropping stretch of coast lined with pure, golden sweeps of sand that are practically deserted for all but the peak months of summer.

Towering above the coastal landscape, the rhino-horn peak of Mount Warning is the first point on the Australian mainland to feel the glow of the rising sun. For all its serene beauty, at ground level this is a landscape with teeth, as you'll discover if you take the four-kilometre hiking trail from Breakfast Creek to the 1157-metre summit. To the south, one of the best short rainforest walks in the country is the track to Protester's Falls on Terania Creek in Nightcap National Park, which begins in a forest of bangalow palms and crosses the creek to a sheer cliff face where a 30-metre veil of water sprays into a green pool. Hard up against the Queensland border is the Border Ranges National Park, a large and spectacularly rugged chunk of the Tweed Ranges.

These hills are also home to small communities of alternative lifers, the ideological descendants of the folk at Nimbin, which became in the 1970s the laboratory for an experimental society that would get back to grass roots living, reinvigorate the human psyche and generally save the planet. Nimbin still wears its matted hair, its bells, body piercings and its slightly outrageous manners with pride. ✶ ☆ ✶

NEW SOUTH WALES

Mullumbimby

Brunswick Heads

Byron Bay

BYRON AT BYRON

Bangalow

THE BYRON AT BYRON RESORT

LOCATION: North coast New South Wales. It's a two-hour drive south from Brisbane, 50 minutes from Gold Coast Airport and 25 minutes from Ballina Airport.

GETTING THERE: Fly Qantas, Virgin Blue or Australian Airlines to the Gold Coast, or Qantas or Virgin Blue to Ballina. Limousine and coach transfers are available from both airports to the resort. There are also car hire services at both airports.

WHAT'S INCLUDED: Accommodation only.

MAKING THE MOST OF IT: Dress is casual, and smart in the restaurant at night. This is an all-seasons destination and the climate is mild to hot all year round.

CONTACT: Outback Encounter
33 Queen Street, Thebarton
South Australia, 5031, Australia
Telephone + 61 8 **8354 4405**
Facsimile + 61 8 **8354 4406**
Email info@outbackencounter.com
Website www.outbackencounter.com

CAPELLA LODGE

Gilt-edged lodging and food to match in a sublime
position on Australia's World Heritage island paradise.

Five-star accommodation sits comfortably alongside the wonders mother nature has bequeathed.

LORD HOWE ISLAND is one of Australia's secret treasures. From the moment your plane sweeps low over the island's sea cliffs, skims across the surf break that rims the lagoon and drops you in the shadow of two leaping green volcanic peaks, you'll be in no doubt; this is paradise in the raw. Now, with the reopening of Capella Lodge after a total makeover, the island has accommodation to go with the five-star credentials that mother nature has bestowed.

The view through Capella's floor-to-ceiling windows is staggering. At your feet, the ground drops away across a rustling forest of kentia palms into pastures and then rises sharply in a toppling wave of forest and bare rock, a green expanse that ends at the towering peaks of Mount Lidgbird and Gower. If it's a typical Lord Howe Island day, the twin summits will be fleeced with a halo of cloud. At their feet, a bikini-sized strip of sand snakes along Lovers Bay, dividing the mountains from a coral lagoon that plays every colour in the peacock-tail spectrum, from turquoise to lapis to jade.

Throughout the lodge, the style is cool, refined and relaxed – a mood that sits perfectly with the island itself. The lounge is arranged with wicker lounges and banquettes and accented with splashy cushions, while the skillion roof brings the full impact of the mountain views into every corner of the room. The blank sheet of stainless steel is a fireplace fuelled by clean-burning methylated spirits. The restaurant tables are set with aqua-toned water tumblers and glazed ceramic side plates that echo the colours of reef and sky. There's a wet-edge plunge pool set into the deck and a pair of lounges for admiring the view – but nothing is allowed to compete with the spectacle, which is exactly as it should be.

Lord Howe Island is tiny, barely 11 kilometres from end to end and two across at its widest point, yet rarely is so much crammed into such a dimple of dry land. The shallow lagoon on the western side of the island hosts the world's most southerly coral gardens. In the interior are dense forests of banyan tree, which can span an area of 200 square metres with its root structure of soaring columns. The summit of Mount Gower is richly invested with rainforest and most of the lower storey of the island is blanketed by a canopy of kentia palms, the mainstay of the island's economy until a decade ago.

The sea life is phenomenal. In the surrounding waters, warm and cool currents collide, spawning giant clams, sea turtles, clownfish, lionfish, butterfly fish and a wrasse known as the doubleheader, a species unique to the island's waters. The island is also a biological ark, a perch for exotic sea birds in migratory journeys that take them as far north as Siberia. Lord Howe is the only place on earth where providence petrels breed. One of the greatest concentrations of the fabulous red-tailed tropicbird can be found along the island's northern cliffs, and so prolific are the shearwaters that a local hazard is stepping into one of their sandy burrows and twisting an ankle.

In 1982 the importance of the Lord Howe Island Group as a unique biosphere and its superlative natural phenomena won it a place on the World Heritage List. This is an island chock-full of wonders, and as a base for exploration, they don't come any finer than Capella Lodge.

Relaxed, pretty and refined, Capella makes a perfect frame for the natural beauties of Lord Howe Island.

A menu that makes the most of the island's seafood treasures.

BURIED AMONG A forest of kentia palms, Capella's nine guest rooms come in two styles, either single-level Capella suites or double-storey Lagoon Lofts. While the Suites are slightly more private, the upper-storey bedrooms in the Lagoon Lofts make the most of the stunning outlook. Guest rooms have a bright, breezy, beach-house feel. Walls have tongue-and-groove panelling, there's a marine ply bed head and the basketwork lamps suspended above look like inverted crab pots. Shuttered doors yawn open to a deck with a day bed, or a balcony in the case of the Lagoon Lofts. Another rung up the luxury ladder, the Lidgbird Suite has its own spa pool set into the L-shaped deck. Lidgbird also comes with its own vehicle – a golf cart, the perfect conveyance for the island's narrow roads and its snail-paced speed limit.

Capella's menu makes the most of the island's seafood treasures, with kingfish, yellowfin tuna, spanner crabs and lobster straight off the back of the local fishing boats. Chef Crystal Raine arrived at Capella via the kitchens of some of some of Sydney's star restaurants, and her love of Asian flavours stands out in dishes such as the seared yellowfin tuna with soy, ginger and wasabi marinade and the grilled squid, green papaya and cashew salad. Breakfast is an ever-changing medley which might include wholemeal fruit muffins or croissants as well cereals, fruits and smokehouse bacon, free-range eggs and sausages – or lemon ricotta cakes with honey and strawberries that will have you charging up the mountain trails.

Capella's food is stylishly
accented with Asian and
Mediterranean flavours,
and its interiors are cosy,
warm and inviting.

Do everything or nothing at all – Lord Howe caters for adventure seekers, naturalists, lazy-bones and gourmets. The Island's flora and fauna is extraordinary and Capella is the perfect base from which to explore it all.

For a small island, Lord Howe comes with a dazzling choice of activities.

OUTBACK
ENCOUNTER
PORTFOLIO
MEMBER

THE ISLAND'S NATURAL beauty is hugely invigorating. Everyone swims, snorkels, hikes, fishes, cycles, takes up scuba diving or birdwatching or golf for the sheer pleasure of whacking a ball around one of the loveliest nine-hole courses in the golf world. The island has an excellent network of hiking trails, but it takes a local expert to unlock the island's riches. Especially recommended are the tours with naturalist Ian Hutton, a fluent and authoritative voice on the island's birds, geology, botany and history. Most challenging of all the island's walks is the full-day hike to the 875m summit of Mount Gower. After hopping across a beach of ankle-turning rocks, hikers must scramble up a trail that disappears vertically into the forest on the lower slopes of Mount Lidgbird. Next, skirt the exposed south-west scarp of the mountain by creeping along a narrow ledge, face pressed against the cliff with a sheer drop at your back. After that, the climb through dripping vegetation to the summit of the mountain should be a doddle.

Sir David Attenborough said of Lord Howe Island: "…(it) is so extraordinary it is almost unbelievable. Once there you can see five species of bird and 50 plants that live nowhere else on earth. You can climb one of Lord Howe island's peaks, clap your hands and shout and, at the right time off the year, seabirds by the dozen will drop through the forest canopy and land trustingly at your feet."

CAPELLA LODGE

LOCATION: Lord Howe Island, 700 kilometres north-east of Sydney.

GETTING THERE: QantasLink operates several flights per week to Lord Howe Island from Sydney and Brisbane. Passengers are restricted to 14kg baggage limit.

WHAT'S INCLUDED: Breakfast and three-course dinner, transfers and bicycles.

MAKING THE MOST OF IT: Dress is casual. Take footwear for beach and rock walking and a hat. There are no ATM machines on the island, but Capella Lodge can advance funds against a credit card.

CONTACT: Outback Encounter
33 Queen Street, Thebarton
South Australia, 5031, Australia
Telephone + 61 8 **8354 4405**
Facsimile + 61 8 **8354 4406**
Email info@outbackencounter.com
Website www.outbackencounter.com

PAPERBARK CAMP

This smart coastal retreat takes a marvellous stretch of paperbark bushland and wraps it up in canvas.

By the time you turn onto the gravel road that crosses a glistening, densely-wooded wetland to Paperbark Camp, you'll know that you're in for a rare experience.

JERVIS BAY IS the sort of place the locals would rather keep to themselves. A two-hour drive south from Sydney, if you turn off the Princes Highway along the road that turns east toward the town of Huskisson, you'll find yourself travelling through a very different landscape, a patchwork of small farms and forest where the trees lock arms overhead.

These trees are extraordinary creations – paperbarks with peeling outer skins, grevilleas and banksias that burst forth with cylindrical flower heads. Drive on and you will probably see the a rainbow lorikeet, one of Australia's most colourful birds, flashing through the trees, or an eastern grey kangaroo standing by the roadside.

While there are other places that take centre stage – and draw the crowds – the marvels and miracles of places such as Jervis Bay go largely unsung, except by those who know and love them. Drive further and you'll come to the bay itself, fringed by some of the loveliest beaches you'll ever see, but for the moment this is far enough.

At the end of this long driveway, the first glimpse of Paperbark Camp through the branches is of a striking construction in timber, glass and corrugated iron hoisted high among the trees. This is the Gunyah, the camp's restaurant and lounge area. Beyond the Gunyah, among the trees that give the camp its name, are the tents. But this is no ordinary camp – and these are no

ordinary tents. Refugees from urban Sydney, Irena and Jeremy wanted to create a special kind of accommodation – one that blended the essential elements of the pristine bushland surroundings with a taste for the finer things in life. A trip to Africa, where they experienced the luxurious, tent-style safari camps that are a feature of the African bush, provided the inspiration. "We thought, why not?" Irena says. "The climate here is perfect, we're surrounded by a national park and we wanted to keep it as natural as possible. We could transplant the African tented camp experience direct to the Australian bush, and that's exactly what we set out to achieve." In fact, what they achieved is Australia's first luxury tented camp. This is eco-tourism at its finest, one that leaves only the lightest of all possible footprints on its marvellous surroundings.

The Paperbark Camp experience also comes served with lashings of style. The food is sensational and sophisticated, the area is a treasure trove of unique sensations and although they preserve an intimate contact with their bushland environment, the tents brings a soft touch to the heart of the wilderness. Spend a few nights under canvas here and you'll experience something special. This is a window on a remarkable landscape, and the no less remarkable plants and animals of Australia.

While the rooms at the camp are open to the sights, sounds and smells of the surrounding forest, the meals add a sparkle to the fine local produce.

Food that is applauded by the gourmet bibles – with accommodation to match.

FOOD HAS ALWAYS been an important part of the Paperbark Camp experience. Almost single-handedly, the camp's restaurant, the Gunyah, has provided gourmands with a reason to gallop south to Jervis Bay, a smart showcase for local ingredients such as Jervis Bay mussels, tuna, oysters, kingfish and kangaroo, often infused with a delicate Asian touch by the camp's expert chefs. Many of the restaurant's herbs and vegetables come from the local farms – a treat for fresh food addicts.

Blending perfectly with the olive-hued leaves and grey trunks of the spotted gums and paperbarks, the tents at Paperbark Camp are all but invisible in their forest home.

Imported from South Africa, the sturdy, handsome, high-ceilinged tents are elevated on their own platforms. Inside, within a cocoon of insect-proof netting, there's plenty of room for the king or queen-size beds and bush-style furnishings, a clothes rack and bathrobes. There's even an ensuite bathroom on the deck out the back, where you shower al fresco beneath the forest canopy, screened by a chin-high wall.

Minimum impact is key here. The tents have solar-powered lighting, and only a small number of trees were sacrificed to make way for the accommodation. So dense is the bushland that you have to look hard to locate another tent from your own.

Life is a cruise – either self-propelled or aboard the local dolphin-watch vessels. The beaches of Jervis Bay – one of the reasons that Australia still calls itself 'The Lucky Country'.

"DO IT ALL or nothing at all" runs the slogan at Paperbark Camp, and while the camp is perfectly equipped for relaxation, Jervis Bay is packed with natural wonders too compelling to ignore.

A relatively low population, an abundance of bushland and several national parks have made the Jervis Bay region a natural refuge for many Australian animals, including kangaroos, wallabies, echidnas and wombats. The local birdlife is superb, there are kayaks and canoes for trips along Currambene Creek to the nearby coastal town of Huskisson, and the beaches in this part of the world are one of the reasons that Australia still calls itself 'The Lucky Country'.

The stylish enclave of Hyams Beach has the world's whitest sand, according to the *Guinness Book of Records*, yet this is just one of a string of pearly crescents that line the curve of the bay. Dolphins often surf in the breaking waves, migrating humpback whales are frequently seen off the bay, and whale and dolphin-watch cruises are one of the staples of the local tourism industry. For scuba divers, the bay has some of the best diving south of Sydney.

At its southern end, Jervis Bay is enclosed by the broadaxe blade of Booderee National Park. This is one of the wonders of New South Wales, a pristine coastal wilderness that has survived in all its glory. From Wreck Bay village on Summercloud Bay in the park's south, a walking trail circles the peninsula to St Georges Head, passing a succession of secret beaches, cliffs and forests of blackbutt, ti-tree and mahogany. Take along a picnic lunch, or better still, take a walking tour with Barry Moore. Barry is a member of the local Wadi Wadi people and his perspective is unique. To Barry, this landscape is an open book. Its minutiae – ant tracks, the yabbies in the creek, the tenor of the wind – are signposts that he reads and interprets as fluently as the words on a page.

NEW SOUTH WALES

Wollongong

Hume Highway

Kiama

Nowra

PAPERBARK CAMP ■ Huskisson
Jervis Bay

Princes Highway

TASMAN SEA

● Batemans Bay

PAPERBARK CAMP

LOCATION: Near the coast at Jervis Bay, 175 kilometres south of Sydney.

GETTING THERE: About a two and-a-half hour drive south of Sydney via the Princes Highway. Turn off at Woollamia Road en route to Husskison.

WHAT'S INCLUDED: Breakfast, mountain bikes, canoes.

MAKING THE MOST OF IT: Summers are warm and perfect for enjoying the beaches and other aquatic attractions, while the mild winters are typically sunny and ideal for bushwalking.

CONTACT: Outback Encounter
33 Queen Street, Thebarton
South Australia, 5031, Australia
Telephone + 61 8 **8354 4405**
Facsimile + 61 8 **8354 4406**
Email info@outbackencounter.com
Website www.outbackencounter.com

GLEN ISLA HOUSE

There are many reasons to visit Phillip Island – the crowning glory being this magical guesthouse.

Set on two acres within the town of Cowes, Glen Isla House is a wonderful meld of the historic and the indulgent just minutes from the coast.

Everything about Glen Isla is beautifully
and thoughtfully composed.

AS YOU ENTER the grounds of Glen Isla
House, the initial sense is of surprised pleasure.
There is nothing on the outside of the substantial
boundary walls to indicate that you will be
greeted by a grand drive where great oak trees
rise in majestic calm above the roof lines of
weather-boarded dwellings and occasional figures
of classic and modern statuary emerge from the
luscious green of formal gardens. In a step 'out of
time' rather than 'back in time', at Glen Isla the
frantic pace of the modern world is suspended in
a sanctuary of taste and artistic sensibility. This is
the perfect place for relaxation, recuperation or
romance.

All this would be very appealing if it were buried
deep in the rural labyrinth of the outback, but what
makes Glen Isla remarkable – indeed, unique – is
that it is sited in the heart of the bustling township
of Cowes on Phillip Island, just a two-hour drive
from Melbourne's international airport.

Glen Isla's owners and managers are
Madeleine and Ian Baker. They lived and travelled

overseas for many years, staying in small luxury
hotels, chateaux and the best guesthouses. From
these experiences, the concept arose to create
the very finest accommodation with absolute
privacy and great food and wine.

"Glen Isla's biggest asset is Madeleine,"
confides Ian. "She is so vivacious and
entertaining; she makes everyone feel
welcome." And some time later, Madeleine
asserts, "Of course, the best thing about Glen
Isla is Ian. He is so cheerful, just so good at
things, and he never gets flustered" – or words
to that effect!

As well as their partnership, the Bakers bring
another asset to Glen Isla – they are financially
comfortable, so Glen Isla operates without any
sense of 'selling' pressure that can afflict lesser
establishments. This means that the level of
service is exactly calibrated to the requirement
of the guest, adding to a sense of ease and the
potential for relaxation: if you want something,
well, that's fine; if you don't, well, that's fine too. ↘

With the owners' penchant for fine food and wine, inevitably Glen Isla has become synonymous with superb cuisine.

With Ian's passion for food, every meal is a feast, with the menu varying to incorporate local produce. As far as accommodation is concerned, the jewel in the Glen Isla crown is the Anderson Suite Cottage.

ONE OF THE oldest houses on Phillip Island, the original two-storey timber home at Glen Isla was built about 1870 by Scottish immigrants, the Andersons. Glen Isla was then a large working farm, but over time as the town around it grew, the landholding was reduced by local development. Since they bought it several years ago, the Bakers have acquired adjoining properties to make two acres of magnificent landscaped gardens around the original house, which they have restored to its original glory and occupy as their family home.

Opposite, is the modern Glen Isla House, designed by an architect to harmonise with its surroundings and offering five-star hotel B&B-style accommodation comprising a restaurant/dining room and six guest rooms. Each room is wonderfully appointed around a particular theme. There is the Oriental Room, the French Room and the Blue Room. Nearby is the fully-provisioned two-bedroom Gate Cottage for self-caterers, but the jewel in the crown is the Anderson Suite Cottage. This separate accommodation has been reinstated from one of the gabled ends of the original house that blew off in a particularly ferocious storm. It is complete with four-poster bed, gas-log fire and a spa bath – perfect accommodation for a sensualist (or two) with a taste for history. All of this, just a two-minute walk from the beach and a 15-minute stroll to the centre of town.

Ian has three equally strong passions: his Harley motorbike, food and, as an enthusiast of more than 25 years, fine wine. Understandably, Glen Isla maintains an exceptional cellar. Ian has visited wine regions all over the world to add to his collection, which he stores in a purpose-built, climate-controlled cellar, the design of which was inspired by the chicory barns for which Phillip Island was once renowned. Ian has nearly completed formal training as a chef, and both his sons are already fully qualified. One, Martin, is part of the team, so it is not surprising that food is a passion at Glen Isla.

Served in the dining room or on the verandah overlooking the gardens, breakfast is a special meal of free-range eggs, sun-ripened tomatoes grilled with herbs from the garden, sautéed field mushrooms and hand-sliced smoked bacon. The menu for table d'hôte dinner varies to include available local produce and ingredients, much of it organic, and to accommodate guests' dietary requirements. All stocks and sauces are made in the kitchen.

A typical starter consists of a champagne terrine or a grilled Tasmanian salmon. A main course could be prime Phillip Island lamb fillets, resting on sweet-potato mash accompanied by a blueberry jus with dessert of a creme brulee, strawberries and Leongatha blueberries. Each course, of course, features an appropriate wine. ↘

You haven't seen Phillip Island until you witness the dusk penguin parade – a heartwarming experience you won't easily forget.

Local wildlife features strongly on Phillip Island, whether it's the koalas, the fur seals, the birdlife or, most famously, the little penguins that march up the beach at dusk every evening.

RECREATION ON PHILLIP ISLAND offers many choices. You can do a lap in a V8 Supercar on the island's grand prix circuit; you can walk along miles of rugged natural coastline or visit the Southern Hemisphere's largest fur seal colony off the Nobbies; you can get up close and cuddly at the Koala Conservation Centre; surf or learn to surf at Shelley Beach and Cat Bay; birdwatch along the boardwalks in the Rhyll wetlands or from purpose-built hides at Swan lake; go parasailing off the Cowes sandy beach or fly over the entire island from the Phillip Island airstrip.

But, if you haven't experienced the The Ultimate Penguin Experience, you haven't experienced Phillip Island. A group of no more than 10 people assemble on a private and secluded beach accompanied by a ranger, as knowledgeable about the world's smallest penguins (little penguins, as they are known) as he or she is entertaining in telling their story. The suspense is tangible as the dusk gathers until these astonishing little 'battlers' appear miraculously from the sea to march up the beach, studiously ignoring the humans equipped with the latest in hi-tech night vision equipment. Truly, a case of the sublime meeting the incredulous.

Of course, there is always the option of a professional aromatherapy massage in the serenity of your own room at Glen Isla – not a bad way to limber up for an evening with such welcoming hosts and an opportunity for exquisite self-indulgence.

MELBOURNE

VICTORIA

Dandenong

Cranbourne

Mt Gippsland Highway

Hastings

FRENCH ISLAND

Mornington Peninsula

Cowes

GLEN ISLA

San Remo

PHILIP ISLAND

GLEN ISLA HOUSE

LOCATION: 185 kilometres from Melbourne.

GETTING THERE: From Melbourne, it's a two-hour drive to Phillip Island, which is linked to the mainland by a bridge.

WHAT'S INCLUDED: Accommodation and breakfast.

MAKING THE MOST OF IT: Take sturdy footwear and comfortable clothes, hat, sunglasses and a small rucksack to carry a water bottle. While warm clothing is needed in the winter months, lighter clothing will suffice in summer, with the addition of sunscreen and a broad-brimmed hat.

CONTACT: Outback Encounter
33 Queen Street, Thebarton
South Australia, 5031, Australia
Telephone + 61 8 **8354 4405**
Facsimile + 61 8 **8354 4406**
Email info@outbackencounter.com
Website www.outbackencounter.com

MERINGA SPRINGS

This sumptuous retreat in the Grampians is
testimony that excellence always prevails.

"WE BUILT FOR quality, not for price," says Paul Widmer as he sketches out the philosophy behind Meringa Springs, a sumptuous retreat that he and his wife Gail have created on the border of the Grampians National Park, a scenic three-hour drive west of Melbourne. First impressions confirm he is right, and so does the fact that though they only opened in summer 2003, Meringa Springs has catapulted into the Conde Nast Traveler list of the 116 best new hotels in the world.

The main lodge, sited at the top of a small hill, and the four villas, further down the gentle slope, enjoy an uninterrupted view to the mountain across extensive grounds with a large dam and prominent gazebo near the boundary fence. The buildings are designed to harmonise with their setting, the outline of the lodge mirroring the silhouette of the mountain, natural materials of stone, tile and wood contrasting with the flimsy ephemera of much modern architecture and reflecting the sense of passive permanence of the mountain itself. The low profile and the terracotta and light olive exterior on the adobe-type walls evoke something of a Spanish hamlet, clustering in a Pyrenean valley.

But, if there could be even a moment's doubt, the hundred or so eastern grey kangaroos relaxing at dawn and dusk on a lawn cut finer than any bowling green serve as a reminder that Meringa Springs is well and truly in the Australian bush. This same mob has enjoyed the luscious buds of Paul's native garden, an intrusion he has learned to control by an ingenious and straight forward adaptation. "Now, we only plant what they don't like," he explains simply.

Paul is as excellent a host as he is enigmatic. Imagine the appearance of a more youthful Walter Matthau, add a trace of the Germanic accent that is a legacy of his Swiss youth, and you have something of the externals of this self-effacing character, but little to suggest the range of talents that he has combined to produce this superb country accommodation. Until August 2005, when he sold his last beloved aircraft, Paul ran a flight touring company that took travellers into some of Australia's remotest outback. This appreciation of the pristine – he is nostalgic for the time when the Kimberley was not so "crowded" – has left a legacy that directly benefits his guests. He has restricted the number of villas to just four to maintain each as an exclusive oasis of privacy and peace. In addition to his skills as a pilot, Paul is an excellent chef, an accomplished pianist, and is responsible for the concept and design of Meringa Springs. Gail's talent is obvious in the interior design and the casual acquisition of a delightful variety of craft works and art that augment the generous spaces and seal the sense of style. ⬂

The lodge is an oasis of privacy and peace next door to the Grampians National Park. The interiors reflect the influence of Gail Widmark, who chose the craft works and art throughout.

A touch of Europe in a distinctly Australian setting, supplemented by exquisite individuality.

EVERYTHING FROM THE broad-brush to the minute and particular, says 'quality' at Meringa Springs. In the lodge, an upright piano sits at the apex where three areas converge – the Windows Restaurant, its fine furniture crafted from native red gum by local craftsman Tim Butler; a lounge with a windowed wall to soak up the mountain views; and a bar of polished and rough hewn 'Adelaide black' granite, a perfect vantage point to enjoy the spectacular sunsets and sample an arcane European aperitif like a Swiss Appenzeller.

In the villas, each entrance lobby has ample storage and luggage racks with inlaid runners in contrasting wood. The bathroom has a full spa, double vanity basins and a twin shower unit large enough to contain any spillage without a closing door. The mosaic on the floor of the shower suggests the gravel bed of a country stream, and this motif is picked up in the centre of the bathroom as an attractive abstracted design. Sliding wooden window shutters with louvered blinds, linen chest and sealed wooden floors, and an elegant lamp, leave the minimalist bedroom free from clutter or fuss, with function and form entwined in an embrace that is the essence of style.

In the lounge, the fireplace with a Travertine marble surround in peach matches the comfortable furniture. A polished granite mini-bar area, though it has a sink and kettle, has no cooking facilities. And why would it, when such an appealing breakfast and dinner can be enjoyed at the lodge – and the chef is Paul Widmer?

It's interesting how the creativity of a gifted individual can be expressed in apparently unrelated forms and yet sustain an identifiable 'signature'. The addition of primavera (a Swiss collection of piquant herbs) adds a hint of exoticism to a scrambled egg and bacon breakfast. Dinner is chosen from an eclectic repertoire of international and Australian cuisine. A typical entrée of smoked salmon, cucumber spaghetti, topped with a soft-poached egg and marinated asparagus could be followed by main course featuring locally-produced Portland beef eye fillet, with a reduced wine sauce and a potato gratin. Excellent wines are available from a generous list. Here, there is an extra dimension added to relaxation, because you can be confident that at Meringa Springs, life is just about as good as it can be.

The four villas exude quality and reflect Paul Widmer's personal 'signature', as does the wonderful food served.

THE 167,000 HECTARES of the Grampians National Park is a treasure-trove of the Australian bush and it starts virtually as you leave Meringa Springs. The park is famous for its massive rock outcrops, deep gorges, waterfalls and wildflowers, between deep covers of eucalypt forest, and a fascinating range of native Australian wildlife. If you are awake to enjoy the sunrise, you will hear the birds as they serenade the dawn, an introduction to the many species that inhabit the park. This abundance includes nectar-feeding birds, the powerful owl and that Aussie icon, the emu. Naturally, walking is an age-old pastime through Victoria's most accessible wilderness and Meringa Springs is close to a network of well-maintained tracks.

A number of organisations offer guides and instructors for rockclimbing, abseiling, horseriding or bespoke adventure tours. Later, when in a more self-indulgent mood, it's just a short stroll to the Lodge, where you can enjoy excellent food and – on a Wednesday – be entertained by Paul and his fellow musicians.

There are some places, and they are rare, where you discover with delight, that everything is simply as you would wish it to be – Meringa Springs is one of those places.

Flora and fauna are just the start. The Grampians' scenery makes you want to put on your hiking boots and get out there.

Kangaroos relax on the lawn in front of the low-profile buildings that mirror the Grampians backdrop. Paul Widmer is an excellent host with musical – among many other – talents.

VICTORIA

Horsham

Wartook   Stawell

MERINGA   Halls Gap
SPRINGS

Grampians
National Park

MERINGA SPRINGS

LOCATION: About three hours drive west of Melbourne on the border of Grampians National Park.

GETTING THERE: From Melbourne, head towards Horsham via Ararat. Turn off at Halls Gap. If you want to fly in, Horsham Aerodrome is half-an-hour away.

WHAT'S INCLUDED: Continental breakfast served in Windows Restaurant.

MAKING THE MOST OF IT: Sturdy footwear, comfortable clothes, hat, sunglasses and a small rucksack to carry a water bottle.

CONTACT: Outback Encounter
33 Queen Street, Thebarton
South Australia, 5031, Australia
Telephone + 61 8 **8354 4405**
Facsimile + 61 8 **8354 4406**
Email info@outbackencounter.com
Website www.outbackencounter.com

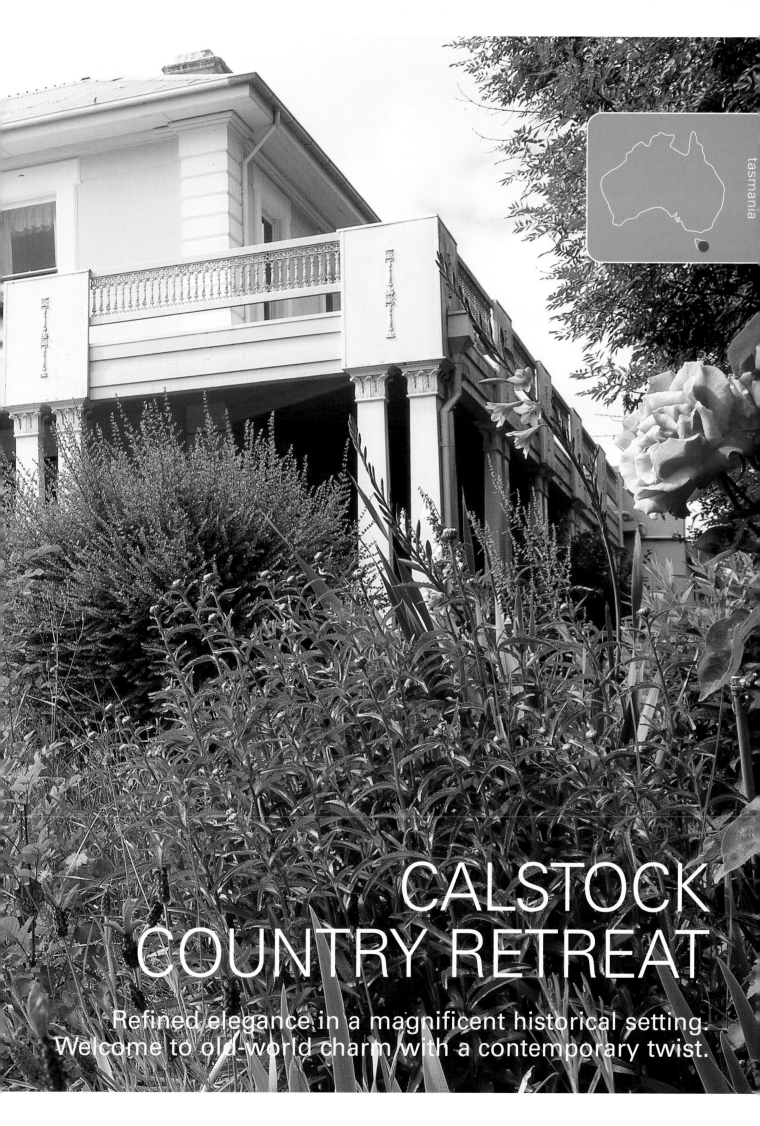

tasmania

CALSTOCK
COUNTRY RETREAT

Refined elegance in a magnificent historical setting.
Welcome to old-world charm with a contemporary twist.

In the soft and downy landscape of Tasmania
Calstock is a house with a pedigree.

Rémi and Ginette Bancal have
breathed new life into Calstock,
a Georgian manor house that
exudes classical style.

RISING IN THE distance is a gracious pink and white Georgian manor house that sits serenely in quietly majestic surroundings, with meadows at its feet and a wall of trees behind. Its breeding is obvious. You've chosen well. This is a house with a pedigree.

At the end of the serpentine drive, pull up at the colonnaded verandah and it gets even better. Here's chef and host Rémi Bancal, grinning as he comes through the door from the kitchen and bringing with him a draught of delicious smells. If you haven't already, now is the time to book in for dinner.

Inside, the house confirms the promises made by the exterior. This is from another era, a cool and patrician world of grand dimensions and high ceilings, and Oriental rugs scattered across softly glowing timber floors. There's cedar everywhere – in the wall panelling, the staircase, the doors and the skirting boards. Vast windows frame views of dipping hills. Despite its mid-19th century origins, Calstock has thoroughly modern tastes. In the lounge, striped

silk couches in cherry and gold sit front of the marble fireplace, while the dining room walls are decorated with a fruit fantasy by Giuseppe Arcimboldo and giant still-life paintings.

The team responsible for breathing new life into Calstock is Rémi and Ginette Bancal, who bring formidable credentials to the task. After a decade as sommelier and maitre d' at The Ritz in Paris, the ebullient Rémi worked as sommelier at a string of illustrious restaurants in Sydney and Melbourne.

Calstock is located just south of the town of Deloraine, in the lush, rolling hills of northern Tasmania. Although it's less than an hour's drive from Launceston, which has direct flights from Sydney and Melbourne, this is a very different place from mainland Australia. The landscape is soft and downy, the tallest buildings in the towns are the church steeples and the area has a rich history that dates back to the earliest days of settlement. If that's not enough, both the Promised Land and Paradise are nearby, but then you might already have guessed.

Four individually-themed
suites set the tone for the
best of country living.

Rémi has an outstanding whisky collection and a
penchant for sourcing the finest produce from
Calstock's rich agricultural neighbourhood.
While the house dates back to the mid-19th century,
it has been animated with a dashing colour scheme.

THERE ARE JUST four guest rooms, all on the upper level, each named after its colour scheme – Ivoire, Cerise, Bleue and Verte. Each suite is decorated in a classical style that owes its clean, simple elegance to rural France. Each room has its own luxurious ensuite bathroom. Ivoire and Cerise are especially outstanding – both huge chambers that dwarf even the king-size bed, and equipped with a big spa baths. On the ground floor, the two-bedroom suite is ideal for family-size accommodation.

Rémi is a chef as well as a sommelier, and his three-course dinners have won for Calstock critical acclaim and a swag of fine dining awards. Rémi describes his food as a "French-influenced, country-style menu created from the freshest local organic ingredients". The poultry and venison comes from the surrounding farms, and Rémi regularly drives to the north-west town of Stanley to buy lobster from the fishing trawlers. Tasmanian salmon is some of the best you'll ever taste, and close by is the truffière of Tasmanian Truffle Enterprises. There are three well-established cheesemakers in the area, including Elgaar Farm, the source of the cream,

mascarpone, yoghurt and low-fat milk in old-fashioned glass bottles that Rémi uses. There are also superb oysters from Coles Bay, mussels and farmed scallops. Goat cheese comes from the town of Bothwell, and local organically-grown raspberries, blueberries and strawberries feature on the breakfast menu.

A typical dinner menu might offer a choice of entrées such as marinated Tasmanian scallops with ginger, garden beetroots and radishes, or home-cured Tasmanian salmon with radish salad and ginger vinaigrette. For the main course, the choices might include rack of local spring lamb with lavender jus or roasted farm chicken with shiitake mushrooms, followed by a black chocolate mousse with orange sauce, or an orange parfait with a soup of red fruits.

Rémi's passion for fine wines is evident in the wine list, which catalogues some 200 labels in a showcase of Australia's finest, as well as some notable wines from Germany, Italy, France and California. Another enormous source of pride is his whisky cabinet, which holds an outstanding collection of single malt Scotch whiskies, some of which date back to the 1950s.

From breakfasting on the terrace to hiking through rainforest to Liffey Falls, Calstock is well positioned for exploring one of the most sublime parts of Tasmania.

There's no reason to rush ... you're in Tasmania after all, so just meander, gently explore and enjoy.

THIS IS A country estate in the full sense of the word. Calstock is surrounded by glorious gardens and outbuildings that are a history lesson in their own right, all built with the simple, satisfying lines and precise symmetry that were the hallmarks of Georgian architecture. In the late 1800s, the Calstock stables bred a number of notable racehorses, including two winners of the Melbourne Cup, Australia's most celebrated race. The gardens are a delight. There are roses and poppies and hedges of lavender and box. There's also a lovely avenue of laurels and holly bushes underplanted with tulips and daffodils and woodland plantings of euphorboias.

Calstock is well positioned for exploring one of the most sublime parts of Tasmania. On the doorstep, the craft and antique shops of Deloraine hold the promise of rustic treasures. Both the Tamar Valley and north-east Tasmania are home to a number of small wineries and if the sun is shining, consider the walk to Liffey Falls, buried in a dripping forest of giant tree ferns. If you want something more challenging, there are spectacular walks around Cradle Mountain National Park, which is often used as an icon for the state of Tasmania. Here too, the country drive reaches a climax in the winding lanes that thread through a tapestry of grazing horses and chocolate-brown fields, against the nuggety backdrop of Quamby Bluff.

CALSTOCK COUNTRY RETREAT

LOCATION: Close to Deloraine, 50 kilometres from Launceston.

GETTING THERE: Calstock is about a 45-minute drive from Launceston Airport, which has direct flights from Sydney and Melbourne.

WHAT'S INCLUDED: Breakfast.

MAKING THE MOST OF IT: Tasmania is cooler than the mainland and be prepared for wet weather at any time of the year. A hire car is ideal for touring, and is available from Launceston Airport. Dinners at Calstock are moderately formal.

CONTACT: Outback Encounter
33 Queen Street, Thebarton
South Australia, 5031, Australia
Telephone + 61 8 **8354 4405**
Facsimile + 61 8 **8354 4406**
Email info@outbackencounter.com
Website www.outbackencounter.com

PEPPER BUSH
ADVENTURES

Made-to-order experiences, catering to specific interests,
reveal the hidden beauty of this most precious state.

Private hideaways, rugged mountains and temperate rainforests are all part of the experience offered by Craig and Janine Williams.

This is a wondrous and unique place, and to properly appreciate its bewitching diversity requires a very special guide.

TASMANIA IS NOT like the rest of Australia. It is an island state about the same size as Ireland with a cool, temperate climate and a population of just half-a-million. As well as Australia's most mountainous state, it is also its best protected, with 20 percent listed as a World Heritage area for "outstanding universal value from the point of view of science, conservation and natural beauty". Many of the creatures that disappeared long ago from the mainland can still be found in Tasmania and its trees are some of the tallest in the world. But there is another side to Tasmania: it has a hint of the Gothic, of the wild and untamed. This is a wondrous and unique place, and to properly appreciate its bewitching diversity requires a very special guide – Craig Williams is such a man. His philosophy of life is evident both in the quality and in the success of his tours. "You have to believe in yourself, " he says. "You must have ability and you have to love what you do."

Craig and Janine Williams run Pepper Bush Adventures from a small office in Scottsdale in Tasmania's north-east, an area dominated by agriculture and forestry. Their tours are bespoke and private. A trip can be just a day or as long as a month, with each designed to emphasise the particular interests of a client, whether it's wildlife, beautiful scenery or fine food.

Accommodation is likewise chosen to suit, ranging from hotels to bush camps. The booking is also exclusive, whether for a solo traveller or a group of 20 travelling together.

With access to hundreds of thousands of hectares of private land, as well as Tasmania's many parks, the tour can start and finish pretty much anywhere in Tasmania, but Craig's home turf is his favourite, a place where the many different types of forest give rise to great biodiversity and differing landscapes.

Craig was born 46 years ago in Mathinna, now a somewhat forlorn outpost of just a couple of

hundred people, but at the end of the 19th century, it was a bustling gold-rush town that was Tasmania's second largest. Just an hour away is Tasmania's 'northern capital' Launceston, but, even as a teenager, Craig eschewed the bright lights, often preferring solitary forays into the countryside, where he learnt to live off the land and to value both his own company and that of the wildlife that surrounded him. He fished for brown trout and giant lobster (now highly protected) and sampled bushes and berries to spice his dinners. He learnt how to find his way without a compass through great temperate rainforests and, crucially, he learnt to feel at home in the wild.

Craig is highly sociable, articulate and quick-witted with a sense of teasing fun, as often as not at his own expense. With these personal qualities, his bushcraft and his upbringing, Craig is perfectly qualified to show and interpret his world to his clients, a world likely to be very different from their own.

Pepper Bush Adventures is about more
than amazing scenery – your senses
and soul are refreshed and invigorated.

CRAIG HAS DONE to bush tucker what Ferrari
have done to the motor car. His ingredients are
all Tasmanian, which is to say, the best there is.
His recipes are original, he often uses native
spices or herbs and his combinations of texture
and taste are subtle and varied.

An extensive cheese platter is followed by
Tasmanian Three Spice Trout (lemon myrtle,
mountain pepper and native kunzea) on a salad
bed. Next are Mountain Burgers with
pickleberry and sweet chilli sauce and stir-fried
vegetables with his signature dish, a finale of
Wallaby Tenderloins marinaded in whisky,
honey and garlic and served with a
pepperberry/port sauce, and vegetables.
Naturally, the best Tasmanian wines
accompany these dishes, carefully chosen by
Craig to complement his culinary creations.

Truly, a wonderful conclusion to an
already magical day.

Exquisite meals prepared by Craig, who uses only the finest local produce, ensure a well-fueled expedition.

Tours can range in length
from daytrips to extended
adventures, and are tailor-
made to showcase the
magnificent diversity of
Tasmania's flora and fauna.

OUTBACK
ENCOUNTER
PORTFOLIO
MEMBER

In such a place, there
is a sense of wonder
at nature's fecundity.

A TYPICAL TWO day trip out of Scottsdale, an hour from Launceston, passes through pretty farming lowlands before an ascent into the hills where tree types change steadily from mixed forest to wet sclerophyll to subalpine. At about 900 metres there is a stop at Tombstone Reserve to sample virgin old-growth rainforest, where the pulse of time is slowed to the rhythm of prehistory. In this world of stillness, chilled air adds pungency to the earthy smell of the decay that is a life-bed to the mosses and saplings at the start of an endless cycle of regeneration. In such a place, there is a sense of wonder at nature's fecundity, the human scale mocked by the peerless *Eucalyptus Regnans* or swamp gum, the tallest flowering plant in the world, which disappears skywards above giant man ferns that reach out to fan whatever light has penetrated from the canopy some 80m above.

A descent in the four-wheel-drive brings the next stop at a charming homestead in a clearing surrounded by forests and an abundance of birdlife that includes currawongs, wattle birds, cockatoos, brown falcons, wood ducks and flame robins. In the dams are a population of platypus. Here, for the first time, the birth (or hatching) of a platypus was recently filmed for TV. Next, a steady ascent gives a magnificent view of Jacobs Ladder, still shrouded by traces of winter snow on Ben Lomond, which at 1572m is the second highest mountain in Tasmania. Then, it's back down, through working forests into the Tyne Valley along a succession of ever-reducing roads that lead (via a padlocked gate and a river-crossing) to a shack, from which the top of Ben Lomond is still visible above the treeline. The close-cropped grass in the surrounding paddock gives a clue to the sleeping wallabies, wombats, bandicoots and possums that will emerge after dusk to a chorus from the frogs in the reed-filled marshlands nearby. It's time for the humans to relax too, with a glass of wine while Craig prepares dinner.

There is another treat in store as dusk gathers. With a strange stuttering yammer, and a darting zigzag gait, a small black creature with a spotted coat darts in close to scavenge for food scraps. Now thought to be extinct on the mainland, the eastern quoll (or native cat) is soon accompanied by several others, some with fawn coats, approaching within a few feet of the seated diners.

PEPPER BUSH ADVENTURES

LOCATION: Most tours begin and end at Launceston Airport, but whatever is most convenient to the client is easily arranged.

GETTING THERE: Qantas, Virgin Blue and Jetstar have regular flights to Launceston.

WHAT'S INCLUDED: Pick-up from accommodation or airport, all transfers, meals, snacks, drinks and accommodation.

MAKING THE MOST OF IT: Take sturdy footwear and warm comfortable clothes, hat and sunglasses. In summer months sunscreen and broad-brimmed hat are advised.

CONTACT: Outback Encounter
33 Queen Street, Thebarton
South Australia, 5031, Australia
Telephone + 61 8 **8354 4405**
Facsimile + 61 8 **8354 4406**
Email info@outbackencounter.com
Website www.outbackencounter.com

⊖UTBACK ENCOUNTER

Outback Encounter would like to thank Paul Myers and the R.M.Williams Publishing team, Michael Gebicki and all of the exceptional people featured in these pages for their assistance in making this publication possible. Should you wish to experience any of these outstanding destinations, please contact Outback Encounter.

Outback Encounter is an exceptionally meticulous travel company providing specialised, custom-designed journeys focusing on unique, private destinations throughout Australia. With us, you can explore the desert, the bush, the rainforest or the Great Barrier Reef. Whatever your Australian fantasy, Outback Encounter will take you there – in style.

Hand-picked destinations for discerning travellers
in search of an extraordinary Australian experience.

"The top 50 travel experts you need to know worldwide."
Condé Nast Traveller UK

For a tailor-made five-star experience contact
Outback Encounter
Telephone + 61 8 **8354 4405**
info@outbackencounter.com
www.outbackencounter.com